Guilt and the Search for Fulfillment

Guilt and the
Search for Fulfillment

LeRoy H. Aden

CASCADE *Books* • Eugene, Oregon

GUILT AND THE SEARCH FOR FULFILLMENT

Cascade Books
An Imprint of Wipf and Stock Publishers
199 W. 8th Ave., Suite 3
Eugene, OR 97401

www.wipfandstock.com

ISBN 13: 978-1-61097-542-1

Cataloging-in-Publication data:

Aden, LeRoy H.

Guilt and the search for fulfillment / LeRoy H. Aden.

p. ; cm. —Includes bibliographical references.

ISBN 13: 978-1-61097-542-1

1. Guilt—Religious aspects. 2. Self-esteem—Religious aspects. I. Title.

BS 1237 .A5 2012

Manufactured in the U.S.A.

To my wife *Ruth*

without whose love and encouragement
I would never have seen the positive side of guilt
or the glorious possibility of forgiveness.

To my children *David* and *Beth* and their spouses
whose help and expertise have snatched me from the
jaws of technology
and whose patience and care have made me a proud
and wiser father.

Contents

Introduction

All of us have a great longing to be made whole. We may not be guilty of a major offense, and yet we have a nagging and persistent sense that we are not right. We may treat our neighbors with due respect, and yet we feel disconnected and uncaring. And if we have done something that we consider hideous, we wish that we could erase the tape and start over.

Patsy, a young professor in Michelle Huneven's novel Blame, is accused of hitting and killing a mother and daughter in her driveway. At the time, Patsy was in an alcoholic stupor and had no recollection of the event. She is sent to prison and spends years living in the wake of her crime. Every once in awhile, events unfold that remind her of what she has done. She is shown pictures of the victims and feels "doomed to darkness for eternity, like I've done the worst thing and it can't ever be undone."[1]

For all of its destructive power, guilt is often a neglected form of suffering in our day. It wasn't too long ago that we could get a lot of attention, especially from a pastor or priest, if we said that we were loaded down with guilt.

1. Huneven, *Blame: A Novel*, 75.

Today, the listener may show some concern, but inside he might wonder how we ever let ourselves get into that state. Even a clergy's reaction may be more clinical than pastoral, more concerned about what is wrong with us than about the well-being of our sensitive soul. Guilt-ridden people just don't get the attention they once did.

It's not that people are uncaring. Instead other concerns pop up on their radar screen, concerns like failed marriages or lost jobs or tragic deaths or family abuse, and they take these concerns far more seriously.

Nevertheless, guilt is still a persistent and potent dynamic in our lives. It may torture our days, consciously or unconsciously, but ironically it can also serve as a positive force in our search for fulfillment. Our task in this book is to get an inside and concrete look at the operation of guilt in our lives and to begin to see how it impedes or enhances our longing to be made right (whole). Hopefully, the book will make us more aware of our guilt, but it is not a "how to" book filled with techniques on how we can rid ourselves of what Susan Carrell calls toxic guilt.[2] Instead, it is an extended study of guilt and guilt feelings and a telling discussion of the role that they play in our search for fulfillment.

We experience a sense of fulfillment, if at all, in short-lived moments of life. Fulfillment can and does mean different things to different people, and it can even mean different things to us at different stages of life. Generally, though, it refers to a state or a feeling of completeness or wholeness. It is a time of felt harmony when things seem to come together, however transitory that state may be.

2. Carrel, *Escaping Toxic Guilt*, 2

There are several reasons why fulfillment is so elusive. For one thing, we are finite and limited creatures. We can imagine more than we can actualize. We simply do not have the time or the ability to move beyond the confines of our stubborn limitations. Besides, as we will see when we discuss shame, our dreams or expectations are often excessive and even unrealistic. Our reach exceeds our grasp, and we cannot possibly measure up to, let alone become, what we want to be.

But there is more to our failures than impossible dreams. We also fail to reach fulfillment because we reach in wrong directions or seek fulfillment in faulty ways. We become the victims of our own desires. That is where guilt and guilt feelings come into play and that is the challenge we face in this book—to uncover the afflicted path we leave in our pursuit of fulfillment.

The distinction between guilt and guilt feelings is fundamental to our discussion. Guilt refers to our condition before the law or before society or before God. It is an objective fact about us, a real and indelible state in which we find ourselves. We become guilty in any number of ways, e.g., by spreading lies about someone or by not being there for a loved one who needs us or by not living up to our own better self. In terms of the Christian faith, we are guilty of turning from God, the Source and Sustainer of our lives and trying to make it on our own. In any case, guilt as fact is a real and objective state of what we have done or failed to do.

In distinction, a sense of guilt refers to our awareness or recognition of our state (condition) of guilt. It is a subjective feeling about ourselves, a sense that we have done something we should not have done or that we have failed to do something we should have done.

Ideally, there should be a one-to-one correspondence between our guilt and our sense of guilt. In other words, we should feel guilty for what we are actually guilty of. Often, though, there is a discrepancy between the two, and this discrepancy ought to raise a red flag about our guilt feelings. The truth is that we can manipulate our guilt feelings and use them for our own defensive or egoistic purposes. The sad truth is that we seldom, if ever, arrive at fulfillment in this way. Our problem, then, is not just guilt but the distortion and misuse of our guilt feelings.

A chapter-by-chapter description of our struggle will illuminate the details of our faulty fulfillment and give us a possible way out. We turn first to the nature of our guilt, that is, we describe the three major ways in which we incur guilt (chapters one, two, and three). We turn next to the subjective side of guilt, to guilt feelings, and consider how they function in our lives and how we tend to deal with them (chapters four, five, and six). In chapter 7, we take a more penetrating look at ourselves by dealing with guilt's sibling, namely, shame. A sense of shame goes beyond a sense of guilt insofar as it is an evaluation (an assessment) not just of what we have done or not done but of who we are or who we pretend to be. It can either complicate or complement our struggle with guilt and guilt feelings. It becomes a complicating factor when it causes us to focus on the sense of inadequacy involved in shame to the neglect of the moral issues involved in guilt. It becomes a complementary factor when it works with guilt feelings to expose the fullness of our dilemma and to take steps to correct it.

Chapter 8 concentrates on the positive function of guilt feelings and shows concretely how a sense of guilt can be a road to renewed relationships and genuine fulfillment. We conclude our study by acknowledging that fulfillment in any final or undistorted sense eludes us but that we are not without resources to deal with it. Our Christian faith speaks of a compassionate and gracious God who both empowers and forgives us (chapter nine).

In a world that tends to anesthetize the pain of guilt and the discomfort of guilt feelings, we might ask, "Why in the world would we ever take time to dwell on guilt and guilt feelings?" A psychological axiom says that there is freedom in knowing rather than in denying. David E. Roberts puts a slightly different spin on it when he deals extensively with the doctrine of sin. "The motive behind the doctrine of sin, then, is not to drive in a sense of despair and insufficiency just because one enjoys seeing men [sic] wriggle in agony. The motive behind it is to reach full awareness of the depth of the human problem."[3] Roberts assumes, as I do, that full recognition of the problem is a first step toward its resolution. And we cannot forget that a sense of guilt is meant to work for us, not against us. It is we who cast guilt in a negative light and turn its positive intent into a suspicious and unwelcomed alarm. Guilt and guilt feelings deserve to be put in their proper place in our search for fulfillment.

---

3. Roberts, *Psychotherapy and a Christian View of Man,* 29.

One

Transgression Guilt

There are three ways in which we incur guilt—through transgression, through, negation, and through idolatry. The three ways are not three separate and isolated entities. They are more like three dimensions of a single reality. We begin with the most elementary and obvious form of guilt—the guilt of transgression. We will deal with the other two in the following two chapters.

∼

Betty W., age thirty-five, is married to a loving husband and is the mother of three daughters. Both Betty and John came from low-income families and were interested in improving their social and economic status. To supplement their income, Betty took a job as a secretary in a real estate firm. She was befriended by a divorced co-worker named Rich. Occasionally, the two of them found themselves together with other co-workers at a pre-dinner social hour. After drinking to excess one evening, Betty agreed to let

Rich drive her back to the office while someone else drove her car. Overtures of intimacy were exchanged but carefully controlled.

A month later the same scenario developed, but this time there were few restraints. After that, Betty and Rich arranged to "get together" every once in awhile, even though Betty suffered "great guilt" after each occurrence. She tried to cut off the relationship with Rich but to no avail.

For Betty, like for most of us, guilt is located, if at all, in a deed or a series of deeds. If Betty can cut off the extramarital affair with Rich, she thinks that she would be free from further guilt and could begin to feel good about herself again. In the meantime, she will deal with the sense of guilt as best she can. She will feel some remorse for what she is doing, she may even punish herself in small ways, and she will resolve—maybe firmly—not to "let it happen again." All of this seems like a fitting way to deal with her guilt.

To say that guilt resides in a deed, or in particular transgressions, puts great emphasis on rules or laws, whether they be human or divine. The laws of "do" and "don't" make it clear what is right and wrong, and if we do not obey them or live up to their demands, we incur guilt. The intensity of our sense of guilt may vary according to the perceived wrongness of the deed. But in any case, "normal" guilt tends to follow a certain pattern: It leads to a sense of judgment followed by the threat of punishment that urges the individual to confess and repent and to offer some kind of appropriate restitution. Betty: "After we had been together, I couldn't stand what I had done. I'd feel dirty and was afraid that something bad would happen to me or the kids. I wanted to tell my husband and ask him for help. But I couldn't."

In the 1960s, O. Hobart Mowrer recovered from a breakdown and developed a systematic, psychological account of his experience.[1] He maintained that the basic cause of our fall into neurosis is what he called "real guilt." We violate the social norms and taboos of our culture and instead of confessing the "tangible social misdeed," we try to maintain a facade of goodness. The denial of wrongdoing does not work. The guilty conscience expresses itself in neurotic sickness. According to Mowrer, the only way we can recover, can "redeem" ourselves is to face the truth and acknowledge fully the foul deed. This prompts us and empowers us to go through the embarrassing process of confessing our wrongdoing to people who we admire and respect. Hopefully, it will also lead us to offer "appropriate restitution to the society whose rules [we have] violated."[2] Mowrer's approach to guilt offers us several benefits. It recognizes the important role that transgression plays in our life. It indicates that denial is not a helpful way to deal with guilt or, more positively, it shows that confession and restitution, however difficult, are primary steps toward healing. What Mowrer implies but does not say explicitly is that if we continue to hide our guilt, the guilt may force itself upon us in the form of distressing dreams, bizarre behavior, or the uncontrollable urge to confess.

---

1. Mowrer, *The Crisis in Psychiatry and Religion*, 1961.
2. Aden and Benner, *Counseling and the Human Predicament*, 102

A Closer Look at Guilt

Mowrer is suggestive but not totally satisfying. We need a closer look at guilt as transgression. We find that resource in Nathaniel Hawthorne's *The Scarlet Letter*. Hawthorne's story is an extended and dramatic portrayal of guilt and its consequences, both for the guilty person and for the people who are affected by the wrongdoing. It is set in seventeenth-century Boston in a puritanical culture that was excessively strict in matters of morals and religion. Hester Prynne, a young, seemingly unmarried woman in the community, appears on a public scaffold with an infant daughter in her arms and with an embroidered scarlet "A" on her chest. Though urged to reveal the identity of the father by the town's young minister, Arthur Dimmesdale, Hester refuses to do so. She is forced to wear the scarlet letter as a punishment for her adultery and for the secret she will not disclose.

Among the jeering onlookers is a recent arrival in town—Roger Chillingworth. His identity as Hester's husband is unknown to everyone except Hester. He is not the father of the child, and when he learns of Hester's unfaithfulness, he wants revenge. He suspects the young minister and becomes his physician, even arranging to live with Dimmesdale in order to take better care of him. He is a cold and calculating wit who subjects the defenseless minister to cruel mental torments. Eventually, Dimmesdale, supported by Hester and seven-year-old daughter Pearl, mounts the public scaffold and confesses that he is the child's father. Dimmesdale receives a long-awaited kiss from Pearl and dies in Hester's arms. Chillingworth, cheated of a victim, dies a short time later. Hester and Pearl leave the settlement.

Pearl never returns, but Hester spends her last years there and is buried next to Dimmesdale.

Hawthorne's drama cuts deeper into the guilt experience than we are able to harvest here, but it is useful to us at this point because it is a perceptive portrayal of guilt on the level of transgression.

Hester has an affair in a Puritan society, and all the judgment of a strict moral code falls on her. She is put up for public display and is forced to wear forever the mark of her ignominy, a letter "A." Women talk about her and scorn her, decent folk of all sorts avoid her, preachers make her the brunt of Sunday's sermon, her daughter Pearl is maligned as one possessed of an evil spirit, and her companion in sin lives as a model of goodness and godliness.

Hester's plight seems intolerable, and indeed it is. But, remarkably, she not only survives but also grows into a capable and compassionate human being. She supports herself by her extraordinary talent in needlework, and her handiwork becomes revered and sought after from the governor on down. She cares for the outcast and shares food and clothing with the poor. Though alienated and lonely, she establishes herself as an important, indeed as a respected, part of the community. All the while her dastardly deed is not far from her. It is embroidered on her bosom and enfleshed in her moody and mischievous Pearl.

Guilt exacted a horrible price from Hester, but ironically it became the source of her strength and wisdom. How? Why? Mowrer may point to a reason: Hester's guilt was out in the open for all to see, so much so that Chillingworth could say to Dimmesdale, "There goes a woman who . . . has none of [the] mystery of hidden sinfulness."[3] In a real sense, the scarlet letter was a daily confession of what she had done. Hester "knew that her deed had been evil; [and] she could have no faith . . . that its result would be good."[4] Daily, she looks at Pearl "to detect some dark and wild peculiarity that should correspond with the guiltiness to which [the child] owed her being."[5] And through it all, Hester feels the judgment of, and over time makes restitution to, the community she has offended.

The Ill Effects of Denied Guilt

Hester's plight stands in sharp contrast to the fate of others who were affected by the transgression. Arthur Dimmesdale, the pastor, keeps his involvement nicely hidden, and his health pays the price. He becomes more and more pale and sickly—his body becomes emaciated, his voice more melancholic, and his hand presses more frequently against his heart as though he is in pain. His parishioners, of course, notice the changes, but they attribute them to their beloved pastor's devotion to study and to his parochial duties. They also explain his frequent fasts and vigils as his way to keep worldly concerns at bay. Dimmesdale is a victim of his own denied guilt. His facade of innocence and piety is of little account against the ravages of repressed guilt. And Roger Chillingworth, his supposed physician, does not help. Chillingworth presses, in fact manipulates, to uncover Dimmesdale's secret

3. Hawthorne, *The Scarlet Letter*, 125.

4. Ibid., 82.

5. Ibid., 82.

malady, which only reinforces Dimmesdale's need to hide the truth and suffer its consequences. The only redeeming result of his plight is that he gains greater understanding of those who suffer and is able to address them with his powerful sermons.

Unlike Hester and Dimmesdale, Roger Chillingworth's guilt is obtuse and well disguised. He confesses privately to Hester that though he was old and deformed and devoted feverishly to the pursuit of knowledge, he married her for her youth and beauty without really loving her. He then stays in civilized Europe and sends Hester alone to a primitive settlement in America. When she has an affair, he jabs her with the haughty pretension that he should have known that she would fall. But Chillingworth's greatest guilt was the pursuit of hate and revenge against Hester's suspected companion in sin. He dumps all of his guilt on Dimmesdale, making him the object of endless retribution. He becomes relentless and heartless in his self-righteous attempt to expose the already tortured minister. Chillingworth, not Hester or Dimmesdale, becomes the embodiement of evil. He confesses—again privately to Hester—that he has changed from being a wise and just scholar to being a vengeful fiend, though the townspeople long ago suspected that he was Satan's emissary. When Hester confronts him with his vindictive deeds, he insists that he has done Dimmesdale a lot of good by saving him from torments that otherwise would have consumed him. He would hear nothing of forgiving Dimmesdale, even though, as Hester points out, he might be the beneficiary of it.

Pearl, Hester's child, was an enigma to her mother. "O Father in Heaven . . . what is this being which I have brought into the world?" Pearl is also an enigma to us. She seems to be a product of the evil deed that conceived her. "In giving her existence a great law had been broken," and she, in turn, "could not be made amenable to rules." Or again, Pearl was born an outcast, and she, in turn, drew a protective circle around herself and would not let people get close. Hester saw these traits as "a shadowy reflection of the evil that had existed in herself" and came to the sad conclusion that "mother and daughter [stand] together in the same circle of seclusion from human society."[6]

But Hawthorne's portrayal of Pearl is not exhausted by these observations. Pearl is not merely the daughter of her mother's transgression, but there is something more going on. It may be lodged in Pearl's fascination with the scarlet letter. Even as an infant, Pearl glanced past her mother's smile and focused on the glittering scarlet letter, reaching for it with a peculiar look on her face. In childhood, Pearl's fascination with the letter continued unabated until Hester, in despair, wondered whether it was "an innate quality of her being." When she was seven, Pearl formed the fascination into a pointed question, "What does the letter mean, mother? and why dost thou wear it? and why does the minister keep his hand over his heart?"[7] Hester decided not to reveal its meaning, because she did not want to pay that big a price for a child's sympathy. When Pearl persists, Hester becomes unusually harsh and orders, "Hold thy tongue, naughty child! . . . Do not tease me else I shall shut thee into the dark closet!"[8] At a later time, in a moment of tenderness,

6. Ibid., 87.
7. Ibid., 167.
8. Ibid., 170.

Pearl "drew down her mother's head, and kissed her brow and both her cheeks." Then, as if to introduce a "throb of anguish," Pearl "kissed the scarlet letter, too!" Hester reacted immediately. "That was not kind. . . . When thou hast shown me a little love, thou mockest me."[9]

How do we account for Pearl's fascination with the scarlet letter, or, paraphrasing Pearl herself, "What does the letter mean to Pearl? What does it say to her?" Pearl herself may find the question difficult to answer, because she may perceive deeper realities than she can articulate or deeper feelings than she can express. Pearl may not even know that the scarlet letter is a sign of a particular transgression, but she senses that it points to something significant and deep, something that the mother both hates and is attached to. Beneath her apprehension is the stubborn fact that when the foul deed was done, the deed redefined her mother's identity. Before the transgression, Hester was a respected and honored member of the community. After the transgression, she became a tainted and deceptive presence in the eyes of others and in her own eyes. This change in Hester's identity, in the way that the community saw her, resulted in a change in the way she saw herself. The scarlet letter became both a sign of her changed identity and a reinforcement of it. Pearl sensed this and related to it in various ways: She used it as a target, she duplicated it on her own body, she kissed it, and she did not recognize her mother without it. Both she and her mother became defined by it and even controlled by it. And just as Pearl became a living instance of the scarlet letter, so the letter became a living symbol of Hester's and, yes, Pearl's identity.

9. Ibid., 200.

Pearl has taken us beyond guilt as a deed to considerations that we will have to return to in a later discussion. For now, we need to complete our discussion of guilt as transgression.

The Lingering Effects of Guilt

Both Mowrer and Hawthorne, one an American psychologist and the other an American novelist, tell us that guilt is indeed lodged in deeds, in wrong behavior. Transgressions against the law, failures to obey the rules of the game, create a deficit and an offense that require some kind of appropriate action. Some transgressions are worse and more determinative than others, depending, in part, on how the community reacts to the deed. But if the transgression is significant at all, it may have a lingering and lasting effect on both the individual who transgresses and the community whose rules are violated.

This residual affect seems especially true in the case of Hester. Her whole life was dominated by the transgression and its aftermath. What is remarkable is how she fared under its impact. We might anticipate that she would become a bitter and broken woman. And, indeed, Hester became hardened, even stoic, as time went on, but mostly she became contemplative, independent, and compassionate. She sees through the rigidity and falseness of the society around her, and yet is able to emerge as a redeeming presence within it. Her guilt—too obvious to deny—becomes a source of strength and resolve. Hester may have become what she became anyway, without the visible sign of guilt, but that is mere speculation compared to the stark reality of judgment and condemnation in her life. In Hester's case, guilt becomes a powerful tool of growth and fulfillment, even though at first it seemed like a sure path to despair and death.

If Hester witnesses to the potentially positive power of confessed guilt, Dimmesdale and Chillingworth witness to the destructive power of hidden guilt. Dimmesdale becomes a helpless and decimated shadow of his former self. Chillingworth becomes a vindictive fiend who loses life when he loses his victim.

Hawthorne's portrayal of guilt confronts us with one of the dangers of associating guilt with the law, with tangible transgressions. This approach can easily end in legalism. It can demand blind obedience to every nuance of the law and devise a system of punishment that shows no mercy. Hester is subject to the most cruel harassment, and her punishment far exceeds the wrongness of her action, especially if the deed was done in love and not in lust.

Hawthorne also shows that the consequences of legalism can cast a dark shadow over more persons than just the doer of the deed. Legalism becomes a whole repressive and authoritarian system that "victimizes" every person within the system, even those who are staunch advocates of the system. For example, the people who stood near the scaffold and judged and jeered Hester were victims of their own self-righteous hate as much as Hester was of her deed. Their plight may be less evident than Hester's, indeed they may seem to flourish within the system, but in a larger sense the system reduces them to cold and vindictive human beings who can become objects of scorn and condemnation themselves, if they breach the law in any significant way.

Can a guilt that originates in legalism be healthy? Hester implies that it can, but then again we could maintain that Hester stood apart from the legalism of her time even as she was a victim of it. Her scarlet letter came from the Puritan community, but her sense of guilt was from her own responsible reaction to what she had done. In any case, it may be the confession of guilt, and not the origin of it, that determines how effective it is. Whether true or not, a better indication of guilt's effectiveness is whether it attends to the letter of the law or to the spirit of the law. If to the letter of the law, guilt is preoccupied with the rigid fulfillment of the law for its own sake. It never leads beyond its legalistic demands to a higher purpose or to a higher sense of fulfillment. If guilt is attentive to the spirit of the law, it is concerned about the law's ultimate purpose, namely, to protect or to advance human welfare and fulfillment. Hester's sense of guilt transcended the letter of the law and was concerned about human beings, even those who judged and condemned her.

Laws give proper order to life. They protect the common good and enhance the necessary and positive interaction between people. In this sense, a stoplight on the corner is an essential and irreplaceable law in the life of the community. Individuals who take its demands into their own hands and decide to ignore them endanger not only themselves but also the welfare of everyone in the community. Both personally and socially, the road to genuine fulfillment is found within the law, not apart from it. If we stray beyond its parameters, hopefully our sense of guilt will alert us to the fact and urge us to change our ways.

Conclusion

The case for guilt as a transgression is easy to make. If we experience guilt at all, it is probably in relation to a deed or a series of deeds. Even then we retain the ability to manipulate our guilt, either by denying it altogether or by shaping it according to our own preferences. Either way, the violation of what we should do or should not do lands us in the turbulent wake of transgression guilt. But there is more to guilt than bad deeds. In the next chapter we take a look at a broader and deeper way in which we incur guilt.

Two

Negation Guilt

As we have said already, most of us live, and experience guilt, on the level of transgressions. But our guilt goes deeper than that. Often it is not just an offense against a rule or a standard of living. It is an offense against life itself, that is, a thought, word, or deed that diminishes or destroys life, either our own life or the life of something or someone else. An example from my days of amateur landscaping will get us started.

The hedge in front of our house was healthy and beautiful. Unfortunately, the previous owners of our home had let the hedge grow over a good portion of the front sidewalk. My wife and I lived with the situation for years without correcting it, even though some of our friends found in hard to stay on the narrow walk. Finally, I decided to take action. I cut the offending side of the hedge a good foot until it no longer overlapped the sidewalk. When I finished, there wasn't much left of the face of the hedge except bare branches and a few twigs. I assumed that over time the hedge would grow back, leaving us with a nice, well-rounded hedge.

That evening as I walked past the hedge, it occurred to me that maybe the hedge would not rejuvenate itself, that maybe I had trimmed it so drastically that it would never recover. With this realization came guilt and an agonizing moment of self-examination. Had I in effect destroyed the hedge? Had I gone beyond its ability to recover and to grow back? Had my desecration taken away its life? If so, by what right did I do that to a living, thriving plant? The question tormented me as I sought reassurance from the healthy bushes in the backyard.

The guilt I experienced goes beyond a rule about trimming bushes. It was about the desecration of a living thing, endangering its chances of survival. This seemingly mundane situation points the way to a deeper understanding of guilt. Returning to Hester Prynne for a moment gives us another entrée to guilt by negation.

The Puritanical community in which Hester lived made her pay dearly for her transgression, and she herself realized that she had disobeyed a moral law. But her deeper guilt was about the distortion or negation of life itself, not only her own life but also the life of Pearl and secondarily the life of Dimmesdale and Chillingworth. In torment, she asked, "O Father in Heaven . . . What is this being which I have brought into the world?"[1] She was convinced that she would find in Pearl "some dark and wild peculiarity that should correspond with the guiltiness to which [Pearl] owed her being." And the townspeople saw, or imagined, that Pearl might be a "demon-child" who should be taken

1. Hawthorne, *The Scarlet Letter*, 88.

from Hester for Hester's sake. Hawthorne portrays well the guilt that is a distortion or destruction of life.

Guilt Lies Beyond Good Intentions

Thirty-three year old Janet presents us with another dimension of negation guilt. She was loved by her family and respected by the community. She took an active part in her children's school life and had even served as a teacher's helper in one of the lower grades. The members of her church knew her as a caring and sharing person to those who were in need. In spite of her busy schedule, she always had time for her husband and for the special dinners that occasionally he had to host.

Inwardly, Janet was not a happy person. She had a never-ending struggle with her weight and had tried any number of diets. Some of them worked for awhile but in the long run they did not solve the problem. In fact, the attempts to diet seemed to aggravate the dissatisfaction that Janet felt toward herself. She confessed to a close friend that she often "blows it" and then feels anger and guilt for not living up to her intentions.

In one sense, Janet is in good company and she could excuse herself, because many people have the same struggle and manifest the same lack of control. But that does not work. Janet still berates herself and feels awful when she does not measure up to what she should do. The guilt is often not experienced as guilt but takes a more indirect form. She may look in the mirror and feel sick or she may get angry at a favorite dress that no longer fits or she makes comments about herself that express self-disgust. Janet's struggle has many facets and takes many forms, but when she catches a clear image of herself she knows that she is guilty of going against her own better self. She might say with Paul, "I do not understand my own actions. For I do not do what I want, but I do the very thing I hate" (Rom 7:15). With this impotence and failure comes self-abasement and guilt.

Paul Tillich puts the point more philosophically: A person's life "is not only given to him but also demanded of him. He is responsible for it; literally, he is required to answer, if he is asked, what he had made of himself. He who asks him is his judge, namely, he himself who, at the same time, stands against him."[2] In our terms, Tillich is describing the self-generated law court in which all of us live, where we are called upon to account for the life that we have lived, guilt and all.

Maybe we should pause here to acknowledge that there are necessary and even positive instances of negation. The dentist who drills a decayed tooth or the parent who reprimands an inconsiderate child or the civic group that opposes forces of hate, are all involved in negation but not necessarily in acts of diminishing or destroying life. Their intent is to preserve or build up, not to tear down. In the end, of course, any particular act may be a mixture of building up and tearing down, of positive and negative negation, but we will dwell on acts of negation that leave us guilty.

As we use the term, negation is like Sherwin Williams paint. It covers the earth. It is so inclusive of life-diminishing activities that none of us escape. On a physical level, negation ranges from denying a needy neighbor a glass of water to perpetrating violence toward the neighbor that

2. Tillich, *The Courage To Be*, 51.

leads to death. On a more symbolic level, negation ranges from making fun of someone's good intentions to engaging in an outright attempt to "break the spirit" of another human being. We can also incur guilt by failing to respond to a person who is in serious trouble. Guilt by omission can take many forms, as my wife and I found out when we were camping in the Blue Ridge Mountains of Virginia.

Our two children had just fallen asleep, and we were wrapped in blankets to keep out the October chill. We heard a knock on the door of our one-room cabin, followed by an urgent plea for help. "We've just had an accident down the road, and my friend is hurt. Can you help?" My wife and I looked at each other in disbelief. Coming from the big city, we thought immediately that this was a trap. Our children were sleeping and could not be disturbed. I looked out the window, and it was pitch black. Unpleasant visions of what might happened if one or both of us went with the intruder clouded our thoughts. "I'm sorry. We cannot help. Try the neighbor next door." Sounds of shuffling feet ended at the cabin to our left. Knock. Knock. Silence for a moment. Then the car next door broke the silence and sped down the mountain road. My wife and I laid in bed, immersed in guilt.

Guilt in Psychological Perspective

Depth psychology offers us other instances of guilt by negation. Carl R. Rogers believes that human beings have an inner capacity to fulfill themselves.[3] He also believes that in the process of growing up, children develop a concept of "I"

---

3. Aden and Ellens, *The Church and Pastoral Care*, 82–83.

or "me," and this concept includes "a need for positive regard." Inevitably, Rogers maintains, children sacrifice their own authentic "selves" to remain important to, and loved by, those who are significant in their lives. Rogers does not call this distortion of the self a state of guilt, but it is a radical negation of the self. It is a shift from actualizing the self to diminishing or distorting the self. Guilt, then, becomes an inevitable state of the self turning against itself.

Karen Horney[4] describes the self's betrayal, and thus its guilt, in different terms, but the outcome is the same. The self turns from itself and tries to actualize an idealized fabrication of the self. In the process, the self loses itself and spends all its energy in trying to become the idealized person. Like Rogers, Horney, implicitly if not explicitly, posits a fall into guilt. But her real contribution to our discussion is the realization that a sense of guilt can be made to serve a pseudo-self and thus can become a perpetrator of false fulfillment.

However dated Rogers and Horney may be, they indicate that the forces of negation may manifest themselves very early in life, beyond our capacity to restrict them. They also show that what appears to be a life-saving move to remain loved (Rogers) may become a tool of negation (the self turning against itself).

Autumn, a widow who became immersed in guilt after her husband died, takes us beyond the self and introduces us to the relational nature of negation guilt. She experienced intense guilt, partly because the relationship between her husband and her was not good. They drew closer to each other as they dealt with Bill's increased

4. Horney, *Neurosis and Human Growth*, 22–23.

incapacitation due to pancreatic cancer, but that did not release Autumn from her part in the failed marriage. She felt guilty for the times that she had given up on the marriage and had pursued her own independent life. Her guilt was not a transgression, though it was that too, but it was a betrayal and a negation of a relationship and thus a desecration of herself and her husband.

When Bill was admitted to the hospital for what turned out to be the last time, he was asked if he wanted to be resuscitated if he lost consciousness. He responded, "I don't think so." Then turning to Autumn, he asked, "Do I?" She replied, "No, I don't think you do either." In a sense, both of them were answering a theoretical question, because neither one thought death was near. Nevertheless, it was a defining moment for them, or at least for Autumn. She answered as she did because she did not want Bill to suffer anymore, but what lingered in her mind was the feeling that she had given up on him, that she had turned against him and had sealed his fate. She suffered under the guilt of abandoning him and willfully hastening his death.

To this point, we have dealt with guilt when it is more or less out in the open. Janet, Autumn, Hester, and others were aware of their guilt and took steps to do something about it. We turn now to a vague, and certainly a disturbing, instance of hidden guilt or, in clinical terms, of denied and disowned guilt. I think Kafka's *The Trial,* like Hawthorne's *The Scarlet Letter,* provides us with a telling account of our struggle with negation guilt. Kafka's story brings us to a new understanding of negation guilt.

Joseph K., chief clerk at a bank, awoke one morning to find a stranger at his bedroom door. When he asked the man to identify himself, his request was ignored. When he complained that his breakfast had not been brought to him, the man said simply, "It can't be done." When K. tried to leave his apartment, he was told, "You can't leave, you're being held."[5] K. accepted all of these insulting developments and decided to let things take their natural course.[6] Thus begins a circular saga of passivity. K. is reinforced in his detachment by a simple-minded landlady who says that the reason for his arrest is beyond her understanding and that he should not take the charges to heart. K. goes through the minimum motions of his arrest, but in fact he moves on the surface of an unexplained arrest for an unidentified guilt. He appears at an alleged inquiry into his case without finding out anything; he goes with "Uncle Karl from the country" to a seriously ill lawyer and is left out of the conversation; he pursues, or more correctly is pursued, by a number of women, but nothing comes of those relationships. His guilt, whatever it is, is never clarified, and he declares his innocence, whatever the charge. He dies as he lives. Two men in frock coats and top hats come to his room, walk him to a quarry, and plunge a double-edged instrument into his heart

K. is a man who lives on the shallow side of life. He is detached from, and indifferent to, not only his legal plight but also his existence as a person. He does not and will not probe below the surface of himself to find out what is going on. He cannot entertain, let alone face, the guilt of his own existence, and this failure compounds his guilt with the guilt of denial. His guilt is not primarily from transgressions,

5. Kafka, *The Trial*, 5.
6. Ibid., 10.

though in many ways he steps over boundaries, but it is the deeper, more damaging guilt of diminishing and destroying his own emergence as a person. His basic fault lies within him, and it is the Ecclesiastical fault of "chasing after wind" in order to avoid the sober truth of what is going on. "I am totally innocent" can only be mouthed by a person who is completely blind to his own diminished or distorted life.

K.'s shallowness comes out early in the book. K. is eager to talk to Fraulein Burstner, a fellow boarder. He misses supper, puts off a visit to see a friend, and stays awake long after his bedtime to intercept Burstner when she comes home. Finally, Burstner arrives, exhausted and shivering from the cold. She consents to talk with K., fearing that it is something momentous. Instead he apologizes to her, because the two men who came to arrest him used her room. Burstner examines the room and finds nothing out of order, except that two photographs were moved around. K. threatens to have the culprits fired, even though he says that the men used her room against his will. Yet he takes responsibility for what the men did and begs the unconcerned Burstner to pardon him. At best K. focuses on someone else's transgression guilt when in fact whatever is implied in his arrest is of much greater import. He is lost in a forest of redwoods but concentrates only on a miniature shrub that obstructs his path.

A Deeper Understanding of Guilt

K.'s myopia is deadly. He lives in a wasteland where no one is honest and authentic with him. The primary motive of his life is to find someone who can help him beat the system. He lives in a colorless world where shallowness is the measure of his life. Martin Heidegger,[7] a German philosopher, might call K.'s shallowness, and ours too, "inauthentic existence." Heidegger means by the phrase a life that is lived in the everyday, in the "common world" where what one feels and thinks is a reflection of what everyone else feels and thinks rather than being an expression of one's own integrity and selfhood. It is an unreflective life that is immersed in the mundane and is out of touch with the deeper dimensions of what it means to be human. In contrast, authentic existence is being one's essential self, which means, for Heidegger, accepting oneself as a finite creature for whom guilt and death are inevitable parts of being human.

Heidegger, like Rogers and Horney, seems to locate K.'s guilt within the self, making it a matter of inner betrayal or negation. Actually, Heidegger's understanding of self-betrayal is different. For Rogers and Horney, self-betrayal means to go with a fabricated, wished-for self instead of developing the real self. For Heidegger, self-betrayal means to live on the surface of one's life instead of standing courageously before, and bringing into existence, the reality that we are as human beings. In this framework, guilt is a posture of shallow or negated existence. And the call of conscience, the call of a healthy sense of guilt, is the positive urge to accept our finitude, which means above all else to accept our guilt and to face the fact of death.

Heidegger has added a philosophical note to our understanding of guilt by negation. Martin Buber illuminates K.'s guilt from another important angle. Buber, like Heidegger, believes that we incur guilt in the process of

7. Heidegger, *Being and Time*, 1996.

living. He also believes that guilt has to do not with particular transgressions but with our basic human nature. But Buber has a decidedly different understanding of human nature. For Heidegger, the focus is on the individual as individual. For Buber, human nature is decidedly interpersonal or, to get closer to Buber's terms, it is one person being fully present to another person. It is an "I" being there for a "Thou," not in some generalized way but in our own personal and particular way.

Buber locates guilt—primal guilt—at the intersection between persons, at the "place" where they meet. "Original guilt consists in remaining with oneself" in the midst of a relational world. If I am not there for another person, or if I say I am and really am not, I incur guilt. I must meet the other person "with the truth of my whole life." If I don't, existence itself summons me away from "the generally human," the shadow of shallowness, and bids me to enter the reality of one person meeting, and being fulfilled through, another person.[8]

Buber's guilt is far from the inner negation of the self, one part against another part. It is an offense against, really an injury of, networks in the whole human community. Buber's way of putting it is: "Existential guilt occurs when someone injures an order of the human world whose foundations he knows and recognizes as those of his own existence and of all common human existence."[9] In my less noble words, Buber is saying that guilt is an offense against humanity even while the individual realizes that it is also an offense against his humanity and against all humans who

8. Buber, *Between Man and Man*, 116.
9. Buber, *The Knowledge of Man*, 127.

share that humanity. We can call it a negation or a diminution or a destruction, but it is not limited to the self but is an offense against the very fabric of human existence. For Buber, then, guilt makes its appearance and becomes a quality of our lives in the interhuman dialogue of person being with person.

Applied to K., Buber indicates that K's guilt is primarily what persons do to the social network in which they live. K. lives a detached and shallow life, not just within himself but in his relationships with women, with colleagues at the bank, with court officials, with those who would help him, with wardens and executioners. In a sense, he negates them by making them mere objects, even as he is negated by them. The women become available to him only to leave him, the court officials summon him only to ignore him, an uncle urges him to become less indifferent to his plight only to pursue his own agenda, the assistant manager at the bank stands in for him only to undercut him.

K. lives in a world of guilt without recognizing that he is a part of it. Increasingly, he becomes a victim of that guilt, even as he lives and dies believing that he is innocent. He approaches death in the same detached and analytical way. In the last moments of his life, after all is lost, K. sees a vague human figure in a nearby window and wonders at long last if it is "someone who sympathized . . . someone who wanted to help" him.[10]

10. Kafka, *The Trial*, 228.

Conclusion

We are all guilty of negation, for all of us implicitly if not explicitly engage in thoughts, words, or deeds that diminish or destroy life. Our offense can be against ourselves, other people, or God. Our greatest offense may be the pretense that we, like God, are always on the side of life when, in fact, we are never totally free from the forces of negation, not even when we pursue our best intentions. In addition, there is a great interrelationship within negation itself. The self that negates itself also negates its relation to other people and to God. Or the self that diminishes or destroys life in another person also negates its own life. In the next chapter we turn to a third form of guilt—the guilt of turning from God. Alienation from God not only distorts our relation to the Source of Life but also our relation to ourselves and to each other.

Three

Ultimate Guilt

In previous chapters, we have found that we become guilty before the law by our disobedience and guilty before the tribunal of life by diminishing or destroying life. These are serious charges, but they do not exhaust our guilt. We are also guilty before an ultimate reality, before the very Ground and Source of life itself. I believe that a Christian understanding of that statement gives us not only a profound understanding of God but also a profound understanding of our human condition.

Ultimate Guilt Is a Broken Relationship

According to the Christian faith, ultimate guilt is about a broken relationship with God, which we cannot heal by our own resources or good intentions. Mrs. Demand is married and a mother of two children. She lives with an incident that happened when she was a teenager. She became pregnant out of wedlock, and in a day when abortion was not legal, she decided to end the pregnancy. She has lived with the guilt ever since, and at the age of thirty-five she went into extended therapy. In the seventh session, she finds herself standing before God, admitting that she cannot accept herself for what she did. She says that her pastor has assured her that God forgives, but that assurance does not free her from the guilt. "I believe human life is valuable, and no one has a right to take a life. I did. I took a potential life, and I did not have that right." Mrs. Demand tried to make up for her action when she was pregnant with her children. "I asked God to make it terrible for me. 'Pay me back. Make me suffer. Go ahead.' But nothing ever happened."

Mrs. Demand is struggling with all three dimensions of guilt. She feels guilty for a transgression against the law, specifically against the Fifth Commandment. She also feels guilty for destroying a "potential life." But her sense of guilt does not end there. She feels guilty before God for taking into her own hands a right that only God is entitled to. In her mind, she became the arbitrator of life and death, and by her action she alienated herself from God and placed herself over against God. When she was pregnant with all her children, she tried to heal the broken relationship by having God exact payment from her, and it did not work.

In elaborating the nature of ultimate guilt, I would prefer to avoid the word "sin," but I have not found another word to replace it. For all its baggage, the concept of sin is a historic and rich way to describe what we are guilty of in an ultimate sense.

Sin is not a legal or moral term. In its basic sense, it does not refer to what we do or fail to do; otherwise, it would not move us much beyond transgression guilt. On the contrary, sin is a relational term, that is, it says something about our relationship with God, or, more accurately, about our broken relationship with God.

In creating us, God gave us, among other things, the power to choose, which includes the power to make or to break relationships. The story of Adam and Eve tells us that we chose to turn our backs on God and to try to become the source of our own fulfillment. Theologians use the term "unbelief" to describe our turning from God and "pride" to describe our attempt to center life in ourselves. Once life is centered in us, theologians maintain, we struggle with a third dimension of sin, which is the insatiable desire to possess and take in the whole world. Theologians call this pseudo God-like desire "concupiscence."

To say that we are alienated from God is to say something drastic about our human condition. We cannot release ourselves from guilt. In fact, any attempt to do good is tainted with self-centeredness, with our own willfulness. So instead of living and moving and having our being in God, we live out of ourselves and manifest our alienation from God and thereby compound our guilt. This does not mean that we acknowledge our impotence and rely on some outside power to help us. On the contrary, we get caught up in the feverish attempt to make ourselves right and worthy of God's acceptance. The attempt is only a further instance of our guilt. Mrs. Demand was aware of the fruitlessness of trying to make ourselves right: "I can't make myself any better than I am. Either God accepts me or he doesn't."

In saying this, Mrs. Demand is on the threshold of an answer. It is God who will rescue her from guilt, or she will continue to live under the shadow of guilt—the threat of punishment in the short run; the threat of condemnation and death in the long run. The very nature of ultimate guilt means that God, who we rejected, must forgive us and renew a relationship with us, or there is no way out. With this admission, guilt ceases to be an instrument of judgment and becomes an instrument of restoration and reunion. We arrive at a point where we give up trying and look to a merciful God to do for us what we cannot do for ourselves

St. Paul adds another dimension to our ultimate guilt. In Romans 8, he maintains that our guilt is played out not only in our individual lives but also in our collective lives. The forces of darkness and rebellion against God operate in the world and dominate the present age. Paul mentions life and death, principalities and powers, things present and things to come, as part of the world that stands over against God and brings decay and death. More generally, he says that the "whole creation groans in travail" until it is delivered from "its bondage of decay" (Rom 8:22). Fallen humanity is included in the travail. Earlier in the epistle, Paul describes the fate of those who do not acknowledge God. He says that "God gave them up to a debased mind and to things that should not be done. They were filled with every kind of wickedness, evil, covetousness, malice" (Rom 1: 28–29). Paul is convinced that those who continue in ungodliness seal their own fate, but moreso he is pointing to the end result of idolatry, namely, death. He contrasts this fate with the glory that will be enjoyed by those who are reconciled to God. They will receive the redemption of their mortal bodies into immortal bodies (Rom 8:23).

Paul reminds us that we are a part of the present age and thus we participate in, and are a part of, its guilt. Paul also reminds us that ultimate guilt tends to manifest itself as transgression guilt. In other words, sin as alienation from God becomes sins or deeds of disobedience. We can actually use this fact to our advantage. A recent experience in an adult discussion group illustrates the point. The group was discussing Paul's concept of sin, and very quickly they assumed that Paul was talking about sins, about particular transgressions. A few people in the group sensed that that was not correct, but they did not understand clearly what was wrong. The confusion allowed members of the group to bring up particular transgressions, and, of course, most of the members that were there were not guilty of those wrongdoings. The implication was that they were without sin and guilt, except for the minor infractions that they may have fallen into, consciously or unconsciously. It was a clever, and to me a hazardous, way to avoid ultimate guilt. A closer look at the biblical understanding of law and our transgressions would have brought us quickly back to sin as alienation. In both the Old Testament and New Testament, the law is from God and is intended to point us to true fulfillment. Any transgression of the law, therefore, is not the mere breaking of a rule or a lapse of our vigilance. It is an apostasy from God, an assertion of our egoistic will in the sense of doing our own thing. In one step, we are brought back to the basic understanding of sin as a break from God and an instance of our ultimate guilt.

Harold Kushner on Guilt

Under the title *How Good Do We Have To Be?* Harold Kushner offers us another way to understand our problem with guilt and with God's displeasure. Kushner begins with a general observation about how we were raised by parents or by teachers or by society. We were taught, he says, that we need to be perfect, that we cannot make a single mistake without running the risk of losing someone's love.[1] According to Kushner, religion reinforces this notion when it interprets the Adam and Eve story in the Book of Genesis as a story of disobedience and divine punishment. God forbad Adam and Eve to eat from the Tree of the Knowledge of Good and Evil, but in disobedience they ate. Consequently, God was angry with them and punished both the man and the woman—the man was condemned to till cursed ground where thorns and thistles flourish; the woman was condemned to bear children in labor and pain (Gen. 3:16). Adam and Eve felt vulnerable and exposed. They felt that their nakedness was a sign of their imperfection or disobedience, and they clothed themselves with fig leaves to try to hide their guilt.

Kushner increases Adam and Eve's problem (and by implication our problem) by adding to guilt the experience of shame. He says that guilt is the feeling that we have done something we should not have done while shame is the feeling that we have become bad people. The distinction is between doing and being. So when we fall short of perfection, we feel not only guilty but also unlovable and unacceptable. A sense of guilt has turned into a sense of shame; our disobedience has become a negative judgment about who we are. Kushner maintains that we do all of this to ourselves, because we are conditioned by parents, society, and religion to judge or even to condemn ourselves. We take a mistake

1. Kushner, *How Good Do We Have to Be?*, 9

or a wrongdoing to mean that we are bad and unacceptable and that we deserve to be rejected and to live in shame.

Kushner confronts this understanding of the Genesis story head-on. First, he reinterprets the story by saying that it is not about the fall of Adam and Eve. It is about their transition from mere animal existence to human existence. Adam and Eve become self-conscious, moral creatures who enter the complex world of moral choices. Metaphorically, they eat of the Tree of Knowledge and their eyes are opened to the existence of good and evil. In this world, there are no automated, animal-like responses. Instead Adam and Eve are confronted by a multitude of moral choices, and they are bound to make some wrong decisions. Kushner believes that God knows of their dilemma but doesn't hold their mistakes against them. On the contrary, God loves them, not because they are perfect but because they are human and their humanness is respected and loved by God.

Furthermore, God sees beyond our wrong choices and unwise deeds. While God does not like our faulty decisions and deeds, God can appreciate our moral plight and can accept us where we are and can love us for who we are, even as God urges us to do or to be better.

There is experiential truth in Kushner's analysis. Most, if not all, of us struggle with the compulsion to be perfect, and we have a difficult time living with ourselves when we fall below the bar. In this sense, Kushner has done us a great favor by his constant reminder that our mandate is not to be perfect but to be human. For Kushner this does not mean that we can rest on our laurels. Instead he believes that God is on the side of growth and fulfillment but that God also understands our fallible nature and loves us for who we are. Above all, God transcends, and corrects, our tendency to judge ourselves by our deeds. While God is not pleased with bad choices, God "knows the difference between the deed that is wrong and the person who is not a lost soul for having done wrong. . . . God is never disappointed in who we are, fallible people struggling with the implications of knowing Good and Evil."[2]

A Critique of Kushner

While there is much in Kushner's understanding of our plight that I can affirm, there are points where I differ with him.

I do not believe that Adam and Eve's problem, or for that matter our problem, is exhausted by an understanding that stays on the level of transgression guilt. Adam and Eve's basic guilt was not that they disobeyed a simple command from a micro-manager God. Their "fault" runs much deeper than that, and the story of Adam and Eve attempts to give narrative expression to it. Unlike Kushner's analysis, I think a more traditional understanding of the Adam and Eve story offers us a more insightful look at our predicament.

My daughter and her three children were sitting at the dining room table just before she was going to prepare the evening meal. Mika, the small family dog, became sick to the stomach and threw up a small amount of bile on the wood floor. My daughter noticed the spot and said to her children, "Watch out for Mika's mess. I don't want you to step in it." Five minutes later, when my daughter was at the kitchen sink with her back to the dining room, her five-year-old, barefoot son looked at the spot for a second. He

2. Kushner, *How Good Do We Have to Be?*, 53.

glanced at his mother's back and then quietly went across the room and held his foot over the spot momentarily before he lowered the tip of his big toe into the mess.

I do not think that my grandson acted primarily out of ignorance or curiosity. I think that he was reacting to my daughter's command. She had forbidden him to go near the spot, and somehow that made the spot more desirable. In fact, I think the command may have aroused in him a sort of rebellion, or at least a desire not to be restrained by an order. He wanted to assert himself. After all, it was a matter of free choice over against blind obedience.

I have seen the same dynamic at work when I have said to my chocolate-loving wife, "Why are you taking a second piece? I thought you were trying to cut back." I can almost see the urge to rebel, the intense desire to have what is forbidden. And I know that my wife is not unusual. I, too, often want what is not good for me, even if I am the one who is commanding myself not to take it.

We have arrived at St. Paul's point. The law, the command of "Don't do," arouses in us the desire to do. Paul uses the example of covetousness to make his point: "I would not have known what it is to covet, if the law had not said, 'You shall not covet.' But sin, seizing an opportunity in the commandment, produced in me all kinds of covetousness." (Rom 7:7–8). Paul, in frustration, repeats the point later in his epistle, "I do not understand my own actions. For I do not do what I want, but I do the very thing I hate. . . . I can will what is right, but I cannot do it" (Rom 7:15–19).

The fault with Adam and Eve, and with us, is not the bite we take out of a forbidden fruit. The fault is an act of asserting our will, of rebelling against a restraint. It is the

prideful attempt to be the source of our own life and fulfillment and to take in what we do not have or to have what
we are denied. That is the point that Kushner seems to miss
in his feverish concern to make us feel better about ourselves by reducing our problem to a learned demand for
perfection. Actually, the attempt to be perfect may be a part
of our problem, but it is not the sole and basic source of
our predicament. We are self-centered creatures who when
pushed assert our will against the forces that would restrain
us. Even if we capitulate and obey the command, a part of
us still wants to rebel against it and may find all kinds of
excuses to do it.

Kushner is right at another point. The complexity of
our moral world means that we will make mistakes and that
we should not turn against ourselves by turning a mistake
into a nasty evaluation of our adequacy or worthiness. But
our problem runs deeper than faulty choices or nasty self-
evaluations. Our problem is self-centeredness or its corre-
late and logical outcome, self-negation. Like Kafka's K., we
see the world, and relate to the world, with myopic eyes.
We can envision the good, but when we act our actions are
tainted with our own self-interest. At this point, Kushner
should not talk about the God who loves us without also
talking about our self-induced alienation from God and our
need to be forgiven by God. Any talk about how acceptable
we are must acknowledge, implicitly if not explicitly, how
God makes us acceptable in spite of our being unacceptable.

Against Kushner's attempt to minimize the burden of
guilt and our need for forgiveness, I think that a traditional
interpretation of the Biblical story of the fall says something
profound about our human predicament—profound not in

the sense that it is a theoretical or a theological interpretation (understanding) that is superimposed on us, but profound in the sense that it is true to and revelatory of life. It
is a perceptive and experiential understanding of our need
to be made whole (right). We may not be aware of the relevance of the biblical story in our day-to-day activities, but
there are revealing moments when its relevance and truth
comes home to us. When all meaning drains from our life,
maybe at the death of a loved one, we feel forlorn and continue to feel restless until we rest in the arms of a Higher
Power. When we see the pain or havoc that we inflict on a
fellow human being, we realize that we are alienated from
the Good and the Noble or, in Christian terms, from the
God of our fathers and mothers. When we are in a pensive mood and feel afloat on a turbulent sea, we long to be
anchored in a Reality or a Power that transcends our frail
existence. In moments like these, we may realize that we
have created our own abyss. On the level of transgression
guilt, our disobedience has placed us outside the realm of
law and order. On the level of negation guilt, our disrespect
for or desecration of life threatens us with isolation and
condemnation. On the level of ultimate guilt, our turn away
from God and our feverish attempt to make it on our own
robs us of a sustaining and empowering God whose word
can give meaning and comfort to us when we most need it.

Four

Inside Guilt Feelings

Having clarified the objective side of guilt, that is, what we are guilty of, we are now ready to turn to the subjective side of guilt, that is, to how we feel about, and what we do with, our guilt. And remember that ideally there should be a one-to-one correspondence between our guilt and our guilt feelings. As soon as we turn to guilt feelings, we find that we have a good measure of control over them and, within limits, can make of them what we want. We will spend the next three chapters taking a close look at guilt feelings, starting with the experiences that make up guilt feelings.

We met Autumn in chapter two when we dealt with negation guilt. We pick up her story here to help us take an inside look at guilt feelings.

When Autumn's husband Bill became incapacitated, the two of them drew close to each other. Autumn continued her work as the pastor of a nearby Episcopal church, but she was within a moment's reach of Bill and functioned as his sole caregiver. She fed and bathed him, she arranged for someone to take Bill to radiation treatments, she cleaned up his incontinence, and she drove him to any place he wanted or needed to go. At night she slept on the sofa to be near him and available to him, and during the day she checked on him often and made sure he was not suffering unbearable pain. When Bill died, Autumn came to a point in grief where she was riddled with guilt over different aspects of Bill's care. "I hated myself for not spending more time with him, for not being more patient with him, for not providing him with better care. I blamed myself for not being in the room when the surgeon did an emergency procedure on him. I felt tremendous guilt over our marriage, over the many things that I had done wrong in our relationship. I regretted the thoughtless and hurtful words that I had hurled at him . . . I obsessed over all these incidents, loading myself nearly to the breaking point with regret and self-hate."

Feelings of guilt are often a normal part of grief, but the intensity of Autumn's guilt seems out of proportion to the care she actually gave Bill. Her sense of guilt moves across the landscape of her grief like a violent thunderstorm and drenches her with remorse. The emotionally-charged torrents of guilt threaten to sweep her away.

Autumn's "thunderstorm" points to a primary ingredient of guilt. She expresses remorse and regret for what she has done or for what she has left undone. Remorse can range from a simple "I'm sorry" to a deep and prolonged mourning. Regret adds to remorse a wish that "I hadn't done it" or a desire to take back or undo "what I have done." Remorse and regret mean that we are taking responsibility for our wrongdoing. Of course, we can feel remorse and regret for the wrong thing, but that does not cancel out their potential value in the clutches of guilt. Autumn's remorse seems to be a mixture of both responsible and excessive ownership for what went wrong in her marriage, but hopefully she will gain a more rational understanding of her role in the relationship as she goes through the later stages of grief.

Guilt feelings are not limited to remorse and regret. There are at least five other components that make up the feeling.

A Sense of Defilement

Against her better judgment, Mrs. Palmer became involved in an extramarital affair and continued it even though she wanted to get out of it. She hid her involvement from her mother, though the two of them were "very close." When her mother died unexpectedly, she terminated the affair abruptly. She seemed to be doing well in the mother's absence, but soon there was trouble. She became restless and confused and began to have terrifying thoughts of death. She also thought that her mother was "looking down from heaven" and was very upset with her. Soon a "dirty, obscene name" started to go through her mind, and she was afraid that when she got to heaven, people would point their fingers at her and say, "How did she get up here? Look how dirty her soul is."

Mrs. Palmer is experiencing the accusatory power of guilt. She feels unclean and corrupted, defiled beyond any ordinary way to right herself. She reminds me of Lady Macbeth in William Shakespeare's tragedy. Lady Macbeth had goaded her husband into killing King Duncan of Scotland, so they might ascend to the throne. Afterward,

Lady Macbeth starts to sleepwalk through the royal castle, recounting their plot to murder the king. She becomes obsessed with an imaginary blood spot on her hands and is persistent in trying to wash it away. She cries, "Out, Out, damn'd spot," but the spot seems to remain and Lady Macbeth moans, "All the perfumes of Arabia will not sweeten this little hand."[1]

Guilt as corruption and defilement need not take a glamorous form like it did in the case of Mrs. Palmer or of Lady Macbeth. It can be experienced in many different forms, like a vague feeling of self-disgust or a repetitive dream of being weighed down or a desperate need to be outwardly clean or orderly. In fact, guilt as defilement is not always clearly defined as a feeling of being defiled. It can be any feeling that takes away from our sense of being OK. It can range from a disappointing sense that we were not our better selves to an agonizing sense that we have corrupted or lost our selves. Finally, guilt as defilement may not even be about distorting ourselves. It may be about distorting the life of someone else, especially someone who is dear to us. Negation guilt is especially appropriate here—the times when we diminish or destroy the life of someone else, intentionally or unintentionally. We think again of Lady Macbeth. She participated in taking the king's life, and it was this guilt, this defilement that could not be washed away.

Out of the agony of contamination comes the longing to be made clean. "Create in me a clean heart, O God, and put a new and right spirit within me" (Ps 51:10). The psalmist's plea penetrates to the core. The mere appearance

1. Shakespeare, *The Tragedy of Macbeth*, Act V, Scene 1, 116–17

of clean hands or noble deeds is not enough. When we are burdened with guilt, we long for an inner rightness that restores our innocence and makes us "whiter than snow." "Nothing less than a complete renewal of [our] inward parts will satisfy the longing to be washed thoroughly from impurity."[2]

A Feeling of Disloyalty

Sarah, age fifty-seven, was setting the table for the evening meal. She had worked hard all day trying to survive her first week of teaching college students. She was wiped out, but she had made a gourmet meal of chicken and rice—her son's favorite dish. She went to the bottom of the stairs and called for Sam to come for dinner. Sam, who turned twenty-four a month ago, ambled downstairs and dropped into his chair at the table. Sarah and Sam ignored the empty chair at the end of the table. Leo, the father, had died unexpectedly two years ago, but the chair had remained in place as if it anticipated Leo's return.

Sarah forgot the dish of vegetables in the microwave and asked Sam to retrieve it. Sam shuffled over to the microwave and returned to drop the dish on the table. Sarah, with a little chill in her voice, said, "Sorry to trouble you. But my legs are killing me." Sam raised his eyebrows but said nothing. The clock on the mantle split the silence into seconds, then minutes, then half an hour. In order to break the silence, Sarah asked, "So how did your day go?" Without looking up, Sam grunted, "Fine."

2. Aden and Benner, *Counseling and the Human Prediament*, 109.

"I hear there was a little disturbance in the neighborhood," Sarah observed. Sam's jaw tightened, but his eyes remained with the food on his plate. Sarah waited for a comment but grew impatient. She opened her mouth to speak, but Sam sprang from his chair and yelled, "Enough! Can't we have a meal without you sticking your nose into someone else's business?"

The situation deteriorated quickly from there. Sam's eyes bulged in anger, and he started to push Sarah around. She ordered him to stop but to no avail. He slipped on a scatter rug, and she seized the opportunity to escape into the powder room and lock the door.

Sarah was confused and frightened. Sam had turned violent on previous occasions. In fact, Sam's outbursts had gotten worse since his father died. Sarah knew that physically she was no match for Sam and that she could not handle his outbursts. On two occasions she had called the police to quiet her fear and to dissipate Sam's anger. She was told that it may be "advisable" to send Sam to an "institution that helps troubled kids."

When Sarah considers that possibility, she gets very sad. She also feels guilty for betraying her own flesh and blood. "He's my child, my son. I love him." Sarah's sense of guilt runs as deep as her love and loyalty. But Sam's behavior threatens her life and forces her to choose between loyalty and safety. Whenever she chooses safety, even if she is forced to make that decision, she experiences great sadness and guilt. It is the guilt of betrayal and disloyalty.

Sarah's dilemma is our dilemma. Anytime we incur guilt, it may include the guilt of being "unfaithful or disloyal to some significant person or principle."[3] And the disloyalty may not be as simple as failing to do what is expected. It may be the greater guilt of forsaking a person or a principle that is a decisive cornerstone of our lives. This guilt, this betrayal often carries with it the possibility of rejection and a longing to re-establish the loyalty ties that bind us together.

The Pain of Deception

A third component of guilt is the feeling of deception and dishonesty. The offense that makes us guilty may be the offense that makes it difficult for us to share what we have done, especially with those who are dearest to us. Miss Havelock underwent an abortion in a day when abortions were done in secret. She laments, "The most horrible part about it, the hardest thing for me is having to live a lie, even to my family to whom I have never lied."[4]

Living a lie may be painful for two reasons. First, it distorts our relationship with those with whom we should be most open and honest, and thus it increases our sense of isolation and shut-up-ness. It means that we can never let our guard down lest we expose our guilt and end in shame. Second, it distorts our relationship with ourselves. It compromises our integrity and raises a question about our trustworthiness. It adds to our sense of guilt, the guilt of hiding ourselves from ourselves and from others when honesty is a desired value. It means that we live with a split between those things that can be acknowledged and those things that must remain hidden.

3. Aden and Benner, *Counseling and the Human Predicament*, 109.
4. Ibid., 111.

The pain involved in being deceptive creates in us the longing to be open and truthful, but the optimal opportunity to "ring true" may have passed, leaving us with the burden of appearing to be someone we are not. "If people knew what I've done what would they ever think of me?" The quote indicates that deceiving others creates its own torment, but to live a life of deceiving oneself creates great inner turmoil.

The Sting of Judgment

Patsy, a twenty-eight year old college professor, appeared in the Introduction to our study. She had a homicide charge filed against her for backing her car into a mother and daughter, and she was sent to prison for it. One of the primary ways in which she felt guilt was through judgment, the judgment of the legal system but more important the judgment of her own conscience.

Sigmund Freud maintained that people seldom feel guilt directly, but instead they become aware of it as the need for punishment. Patsy, too, expresses her guilt by dealing with the need for punishment. When asked if she would ever want children, her immediate response was: "Even if I wanted kids, I don't deserve them . . . How dare [I] have a child when [I've] killed someone else's?" Patsy's sense of self-judgment is harsh. She believes that the price she should pay, or needs to pay, for killing a child is not to have a child of her own. She goes beyond the need to be punished to the need to be punished along the lines of the Talion principle—"an eye for an eye." Her sense of judgment is unforgiving.[5]

Judgment is part of the larger cycle of guilt. Guilt—punishment—confession and absolution—restitution. If this cycle is not completed, we may stall in self-rejection and live with the feeling of being condemned.

Andy, age seventeen, got stuck in guilt and never moved through the cycle. He is a teenage basketball player in Sharon Draper's novel *Tears for a Tiger*. Andy and three friends were drinking and driving to celebrate a big win. The car, with Andy at the wheel, started to weave across the lanes of I-75. Cars honked at them, but the boys found it entertaining. Suddenly, the car hit a retaining wall. Rob Washington, who was sitting in the passenger seat with his legs on the dashboard, was stuck in the car. His legs were protruding through the broken windshield. Andy and the other two boys tried to rescue Rob, but the car burst into flames and Rob died while screaming, "Andy. Andy . . . Please don't let me die like this."[6]

Andy blamed himself for Rob's death and never found a way out of the quagmire, even though a few people tried to help him. His parents sent him to a psychologist, but Andy resisted help at every turn, saying in each session that he was doing better. Finally when his world fell apart, Andy called the psychologist but he was out of town attending his mother's funeral. As for Andy's friends, they noticed the gradual descent into the fury of self-blame, but they did not know what to do. Andy's father was only interested in a better report card. And Andy's basketball coach wanted to

5. Huneven, *Blame*, 169.
6. Draper, *Tears of a Tiger*, 14.

believe Andy when he said that his grades were improving, that he and his girlfriend were "really tight,"[7] and that he was getting his "act together." On this "encouraging" note, the coach went on to talk about what was really on his mind: The unforgettable impression that Andy will make the next time basketball scouts come to town to see Andy play.

Andy felt like he was drowning. His head was throbbing. His mind was cloudy. His heart was bloody. His soul was on ice. And the only way out was to sleep forever.[8]

Guilt as unrelieved judgment and condemnation dragged Andy into a pit, and there was no one to help him through the cycle of guilt. The threat of punishment and of self-judgment consumed him. His confessions of guilt fell on deaf ears, and his act of restitution became a final act of sacrificing himself.

The Despair of Lost Destiny

After Patsy was released from prison, she went into therapy with a man named Silver. In one of the sessions, Silver introduced the idea of a "higher, truer self . . . that knows what's best for" a person. Silver turns to Patsy and says, "Isn't that why you come here? To find and nourish that authentic, unenslaved self?" Patsy replies, "Not at all. That never even occurred to me." She's in therapy, she says, to learn "how to live with guilt."

Patsy witnesses to the importance of guilt and the difficulty in coming to terms with it. Guilt sent Patsy to prison, and in many ways it overshadowed her life after

7. Ibid., 143.
8. Ibid., 159.

prison. Consequently, it is natural that she would be pre-occupied with the very practical task of learning how to live with guilt.[9]

What I question is Patsy's apparent disinterest in the authentic self. Guilt is related directly to who we are, and it does have an impact on our destiny, on who we can become. At the present time, Patsy may feel that that concern is a purely theoretical issue, but in fact it is of vital importance in the long run. Guilt often means lost, or at least distorted, destiny. That was true in Patsy's life, beginning with the guilt that sent her to prison and ending with the guilt that hung over her like a dark cloud, even after she had served her time.

Lost destiny tends toward despair. It implies that one "has forfeited the chance, maybe even the right, to become what we were meant to be."[10] It is the agony of being permanently bent out of shape or of having lost our way. To feel good about ourselves we need to feel that we are who we are, that we are faithful to what we were meant to be. Any significant deviation from this path can create a sickening sense that we are violating our own basic nature, that we have strayed from the path. Andy was aware of this loss. He dreamed of getting a scholarship and playing basketball in college. As Andy became torched by self-blame and moved more and more into his own imploded world, he could see that his dream was caving in upon itself. "When [college scouts] see my low grades, all my absences, and my police record, they'll break their necks running away."

9. Huneven, *Blame*, 167.

10. Aden and Benner, *Counseling and the Human Predicament,* 114.

Andy consoles himself, and at the same time reveals the black hole that he is falling into, by declaring, "I don't need college. I don't need basketball. I don't need Keisha [his girl-friend]. I don't need nothing."[11] Andy has lost all interest in the activities and hopes that gave meaning to his life.

Our look inside guilt feelings reveals their complexity and power. Before we discuss how we tend to soften their blow (chapter six), we need to consider how they can be distorted and thus robbed of their potentially positive intent.

11. Draper, *Tears for a Tiger*, 145.

Five

Distortions of Guilt Feelings[1]

All guilt feelings are not created equal. There are healthy ones and unhealthy ones. It is important to know the difference between the two.

If our guilt feelings serve the basic intent of guilt, which is to give us guidance as moral creatures, they serve as a healthy alarm that tells us that something is rotten in the state of Denmark or, less metaphorically, that there is a questionable gap between what we have done and what we ought to have done. Violating a traffic light comes to mind. If we go through a red light, we are guilty and ought to be aware of our wrongdoing. In this case, our sense of guilt is healthy and basically serves a positive purpose, even though it might make us more uncomfortable than we desire.

Unfortunately, a sense of guilt can be distorted in at least three different ways, and then they are not an accurate and helpful barometer of our wrongdoing.

1. Chapter 5 is based on a previously-published article: LeRoy Aden, "Distortions of a Sense of Guilt," *Pastoral Psychology*, vol. 15,141 (Feb, 1964), 16–26.

Our Past Can Live in the Present

The first distortion is an instance of Sigmund Freud's discovery that our past can live in the present. This is certainly true of guilt feelings. If we do not deal with, and resolve, guilt from an earlier traumatic wrongdoing, the guilt continues to exist unconsciously and can exert a marked influence on our perception of a present situation, especially if there is a similarity between the past and the present situations.

An obvious example of our point is that Lady Macbeth's recent involvement in King Duncan's death is alive and well in the imaginary blood spot that she cannot wash away. Or again, Autumn's guilt after Bill's death cannot be from her unselfish care of Bill as he was dying, but it seems to be a residual consequence of her uncaring treatment of Bill earlier in their marriage. A more extended example of the past distorting the present is given in the case of John Wells. John spent his early adult years in the army, where he lived a libertine life. He met Helen six months before he was discharged from the army and married her six months after he was discharged. John and Helen settled into a disciplined, somewhat rigid life. He went to the local university to become a high school teacher, and she taught in a suburban grade school to finance their plans.

Helen taught school with a newly divorced person name Joan. They became good friends, and because Joan seemed to be lonely Helen invited her over for dinner one night. The dinner went well, and the three of them shared pleasant stories of their younger years. When it was time for Joan to go home, John offered to provide "safe passage on the city streets."

When John and Joan arrived at Joan's apartment, she invited him in "for a little chat." The chat turned into a "seductive session." When John got home an hour and a half later, he was upset and distraught. He assured Helen that nothing had happened, but his pensive mood did not match his words of reassurance. Nevertheless, Helen believed him, and the two of them fell into a restless sleep.

The duplicity in John's reaction raises a question in our minds. If John was truthful with Helen, why was he so pensive? On the contrary, the strength he showed in apparently resisting Joan's advances should please him and make him proud of himself. The answer may be lodged in the libertine life John lived in the army. The guilt incurred then may be reawakened by his temptation to take advantage of a "golden" opportunity now. And besides, as Freud points out, a person sees one's own inner desires even though they are hidden from public view. So John may feel condemned by his inner thoughts and desires. In his mind he is guilty of wrongdoing, even though he was not sexual with Joan. John's feeling of guilt accuses him of betraying his "new" life and threatens him with the possibility of punishment, e.g., with the possible loss of Helen's love.

John's situation indicates that, however much we deny our guilt, guilt is still a present and potent dynamic in our lives. It can drive us to distraction, it can distort our perception of ourselves, and it can push us into a feverish attempt to make ourselves right. These consequences of guilt can be reawakened from the past as much as they can proceed from a guilt that is incurred in a contemporary wrongdoing.

Guilt Can Conceal

The second way in which guilt feelings can be distorted is that they can conceal our guilt as much as they reveal it. In other words, we have the egoistic capacity to make our guilt feelings what we want them to be. We can feel guilty for a small infraction and use the feelings to hide a deeper guilt. Children use this maneuver to good advantage. The child admits to skipping past the hutch when running in the house is forbidden, but what the child does not own up to is that he or she was actually trying to scale the hutch to get at the candy dish. The antique dish now lies in broken pieces on the floor, and the child escapes the consequences of a deeper guilt by taking responsibility for a less serious transgression.

Adults are also skilled practitioners of concealing guilt rather than revealing it. They live and deal with so many inconsequential instances of guilt that an outside observer could question the value or wisdom of any guilt feelings. The unfaithful husband is liable to explain his unfaithfulness by citing the harsh words that were exchanged at the breakfast table two months ago. The overweight wife may blame the heavy intake of calories on the neighbor who rebuffed her. The teenager may explain his or her poor grades by criticizing the teacher for not clarifying the exact requirements of an assignment.

Guilt Can Protect a Faulty Style of Life

Guilt feelings can be distorted in a third and unexpected way. They can be enlisted to protect, or even to enhance, an unhealthy and questionable style of life. This is the most radical way in which a sense of guilt can be abused, and it means that guilt feelings serve a psychological rather than a moral purpose. They operate in the name of characterlogical needs and do not serve as a barometer of our ethical behavior.

Miss Jade is a dependent, self-effacing person. Occasionally, she will assert herself and speak her mind. At that point, she feels guilty, and the guilt tends to drive her back into a passive and submissive style of life. Her guilt feelings have become unhealthy, because they perpetuate a mode of relating to people that she ought to change.

The trouble may go deeper. Self-effacement by its very nature questions an individual's right to be an independent person. Underneath, it really raises a question about the person's right to exist at all. Negation in this form may be aggravated by someone who continually questions the person's worth or competence, but it can also be perpetuated by guilt feelings that continually condemn and destroy. Miss Jade spent her infancy and childhood in an atmosphere of rejection and negation. Her mother welcomed her birth as a "little catastrophe," and in her childhood Miss Jade came to feel that the mother's constant criticisms were rooted in "an unconscious will to abort an unwanted life." Miss Jade grew up apologizing for herself. In fact, she felt that her existence was no more than a "little ball of derived energy . . . whirling upon itself, with its void center." Only after Miss Jade was affirmed as a person of worth by a friend who loved her was she able to affirm herself as a person in her own right.

The three ways in which guilt feelings can be distorted do not serve us well. The first distortion, where a past guilt lives in the present, locks us into an old battle even as it fails to deal with our present guilt. The second distortion, where the guilt we feel conceals rather than reveals, "protects" us in the name of disowning the fullness or depth of our guilt, leaving us with a hidden and unresolved residue of guilt. The third distortion, where guilt serves a faulty style of life, takes us away from genuine fulfillment rather than promoting it.

Guilt feelings are subject to more than distortion. They are also subject to our own willful manipulation of them. In the next chapter, we consider how we use, really misuse, our guilt feelings, and in the process we will see that our problem is not simply guilt feelings but more so what we do with them.

Six

The Games We Play with
Guilt Feelings

The games we play with guilt feelings are not playful at all. They are deadly serious. In the first two games, the blame game and scapegoating, we attempt to escape guilt and guilt feelings by making someone else guilty. In the third game, self-justification, we deal with guilt and guilt feelings by parading our supposed righteousness. All three games can be carried on consciously or unconsciously.

The Blame Game

On Tuesday, May 11, 2010, three men stood before the Senate's Energy and National Resources Committee and were asked to give an account of why there was a major explosion on the Deepwater Horizon offshore rig in the Gulf of Mexico. As a result of the explosion, a massive amount of crude oil spilled into the Gulf and threatened marine life, sensitive marshes, sea birds, and human jobs. It was hoped that the three CEOs would shed light on their joint effort to drill and to secure a deep sea oil well. Instead each man engaged in an obvious attempt to shift the blame away from his company. British Petroleum said that the catastrophic spill was caused by the failure of Transocean's blowout preventer, which was designed to shut down the oil flow in case of an emergency. Transocean said that British Petroleum was in charge of the operation and was therefore responsible, and besides, it said, Halliburton was at fault, because their attempt to plug the exploratory well with concrete was not done properly. Halliburton turned back on Transocean to assure everyone that their work was completed in accordance with British Petroleum's construction plans. The blame game went on and shed no light on the real problem, nor did it stop the flow of crude oil.

The blame game is not intended to serve a positive purpose. It assumes that something went wrong, and it intends to shift the blame to some other person or agency. Guilt feelings are forged into an arrow of accusation and are aimed at a likely target, whether friend or foe. The obvious intent is to free the guilty party of all responsibility for the wrongdoing and to release the person from any implied judgment and possible punishment. On a deeper level, it is an attempt to play the role of victim and to share in all its benefits instead of being cast in the role of villain and suffer all its disadvantages. It is a blatant denial of all culpability in order to establish a semblance of innocence.

We can play the blame game in a single instance or it can become a way of life. For Joan, it was a standard operating procedure to deal with any situation where she felt implicated. If she missed an important business meeting, she would pass it off as the secretary's fault. If she felt that she was not as happy as she once was, she would say to her husband, "I've changed. Your pessimistic attitude must be getting to me." Like the rest of us, Joan incurred guilt in the very process of living, but she seldom, if ever, felt any guilt feelings. She was never at fault. What Joan missed is what guilt feelings can offer: An opportunity to examine what went wrong and to find out how the wrong can be avoided the next time. Joan never learned from her mistakes, because she never made any.

Virginia Satir, in a book entitled *Peoplemaking,* describes four roles that people take in relating to others. The four are: placater, distracter, computer, and blamer. The last one is relevant to our discussion. Satir says, "The blamer is a fault-finder, a dictator, a boss."[1] Inside, blamers are unsure of themselves and don't feel like they are worth anything, but outwardly they are cocky and accusatory with finger extended toward the accused. They communicate verbally and non-verbally that the accused person never gets anything right and that the world would be better off without them.

Satir's caricature is designed to serve a role-playing purpose, but it lifts out some of the characteristics of the blamer. The stance of the blamer is accusatory, no matter how well it is hidden, and the implied message of the blamer is that the accused bears full responsibility for what went wrong.

The blame game may provide temporary relief to the one who blames, but it is a deadly toxin in the moral sphere of our lives. It trades the discomfort of guilt feelings for a pseudo-sedative of supposed innocence. Moreover, it

1. Satir, *Peoplemaking,* 66.

precludes the possibility of change and transformation. As long as we project our guilt onto someone else, we have no need to change and we are in no position to deal with the consequences of our guilt. Ultimately, the blame game places us outside the salutary work of Christ, for where there is no guilt there is no need for forgiveness.

Scapegoating

In general, scapegoating, like the blame game, refers to the practice of putting our guilt on someone or something else, but scapegoating is a more complex and ritualized attempt to rid ourselves of wrongdoing. We will focus on scapegoating that occurs within the family. First, however, we need to put scapegoating in a historical context.

Scapegoating can be traced back to Leviticus 16: 21–22 in the Old Testament. In that passage, scapegoating was a ritual of purification that was performed once a year on the Day of Atonement. Aaron, the high priest, put all the iniquities of the Israelites on the head of a live goat. The goat was led into the wilderness and released, freeing the Israelites from all their transgressions. This ritual and symbolic act had four major characteristics: It was a conscious and intentional act that took place once a year. It was a community and cultic act that promoted a sense of fellowship among the people. It dealt with, and got rid of, guilt and indirectly guilt feelings. And, finally, it addressed and renewed Israel's relationship with God.

Family scapegoating as practiced today is the exact opposite of these four characteristics: It is often not a conscious act on the part of either the perpetrators or the victim. It is a family and individual affair that provides a sense of fellowship to only selected members of the family. It is a way to deal with guilt feelings more than it is with guilt; in fact, it may be used to address many other family problems besides guilt. And, finally, it has little to do with our relationship with God and has everything to do with relationships and problems within the family.

Family scapegoating is a sacrificial system, a network of family interaction where someone pays a price for the sake of the family. It is also a system of self-justification where the family works out its guilt feelings (or other problems) and becomes free of them by making them someone else's problem. In both cases, scapegoating is used to maintain family equilibrium. It covers up marital or family tension and excuses the family from having to face the tension or to do anything about it. Instead, the family's energy is focused on either blaming the scapegoat or "helping" the scapegoat, and the family thinks that their problems will be solved when the scapegoat gets it together. In this sense, if guilt is the problem scapegoating is a systematic denial of guilt even while it attempts to work out its guilt in and through the scapegoat.

As we implied above, family scapegoating can be prompted by a number of different family problems: guilt, failure, disappointment, anger, the elusiveness of love. We have focused on the use of scapegoating to avoid or handle guilt feelings. Scapegoating not only relieves the family of guilt feelings but also it allows the family to work through them by dealing with the scapegoat's guilt. The extra care that the family has to expend to care for the scapegoat serves as a Good Samaritan way to work out the family's guilt and guilt feelings without ever acknowledging them.

One member of the family, usually the most vulnerable member, is chosen to serve as a scapegoat. The choice is usually made on an unconscious level, but it may be based on an identifiable reason, e.g., the member who is the most "guilty" may be chosen to carry the family's guilt feelings. In any case, the scapegoat bears all the family's iniquities and figuratively is sent to a "solitary land." The scapegoat, in turn, may show greater signs of distress, and this increased stress (tension) confirms the family's choice in the first place. The choice may receive added confirmation if the scapegoat is sent to a professional person to receive help, and this person confirms the scapegoat's state of distress and depression.

Scapegoats have their day in court. Scapegoating tends to increase the guilt of those who do the scapegoating, even when the original motive for it is not guilt. The perpetrators feel badly for their treatment of the scapegoat, and thus they become the victims of their own actions. In this way, scapegoating is not an answer to guilt feelings but a largely unconscious promotion of them. Ironically, the scapegoat has exacted a toll from the people who started it. The one redeeming factor in this is that the scapegoat has "resolved" the familial or marital problem, partly because scapegoating relieves, or at least focuses, the family's tension and partly because those who scapegoat are drawn together to address a common problem. The benefits, of course, may be short-lived.

Family scapegoating has at least one parallel to the Old Testament ritual. It promises to do something for those who do the scapegoating. In this sense, family scapegoating is part of a sacrificial system that assumes that we can be healed by putting our guilt on the "head" of something or someone who then stands in our stead and suffers the consequences of our guilt.

Nineteen-year-old Ed was at the wheel of the family's Ford Explorer. His father George, who had just turned forty, sat in the seat beside him. Seventeen-year-old Albert, sat in the back seat as the three of them traveled along a dusty country road on their way to an auction. Ed was going faster than the country road liked, but George said nothing to him. Instead all three were busy talking about the tasseled corn that moved in harmony with the gusty wind.

As Ed approached an intersection in the road, he caught a fleeting glimpse of a speeding car that was bearing down on his right side. He swerved slightly, but it was too late. The car ploughed head long into the Explorer and shoved it off the road. The father never knew what hit him. Ed and Albert lay dazed for a time, but then they were able to struggle out of the wreckage.

Young Albert replayed the accident over and over in his mind. He blamed Ed. If Ed had been paying attention to his driving, Albert would still have a father. He had just gotten close to his dad after years of rebellion, and now his father was gone. Albert's resentment lasted for years. He refused to acknowledge Ed as a brother and discredited him in front of the family at every opportunity. Eventually, Albert himself became so miserable that he went to talk to his pastor. The two of them decided to meet for awhile to give Albert a chance to "talk things out."

Albert started with Ed. Then he got to the tremendous loss of his father. In the middle of one session, he suddenly started to talk about the accident. He recalled the morning it happened and remembered that he and his brother were "at each other all morning." Albert was upset, because he wanted to drive that morning, but Ed insisted that he was older and should drive. Albert recalled that Ed had became so irritated with his constant badgering that Ed glared at him in the rear-view mirror. Suddenly, the sound of crushing medal, and Albert was pinned against the car door.

Albert starred into blank space. He knew that he had been on his brother's case for years, blaming him for the accident and for his father's death. But what he hadn't realized was that he had played a part in the accident. He had taken Ed's attention off the road by badgering him, and the father paid the price. A sense of guilt swept over Albert and consumed him. A large tear moistened the corner of his eye and dropped on his faded blue shirt.

Albert left the pastor's study with a new insight on what happened, but the insight was short-lived. Soon Albert's resentment returned and he was back to holding Ed responsible for the accident. He was convinced that Ed deserved everything he got.

Albert never owned up to his part in the father's death but instead held Ed accountable. His anger moved beyond blame to scapegoating. He bought into the family's practice of putting their sense of loss and their tangled lives on Ed and expected Ed to pay the price for their emptiness and loss. If only Ed would admit his mistake, and instead of trying to be a surrogate father would acknowledge his responsibility for the loss, everyone would get along better and would begin to work together. Until then they felt more comfortable keeping Ed on the family altar and having him sacrifice his happiness for their tenuous peace of mind

Self-Justification

There is an element of self-justification in both the blame game and in scapegoating, but self-justification can stand on its own as a game we play with guilt and guilt feelings. It is exactly what the name implies. It is an attempt by persons to absolve, or even to exonerate, themselves by emphasizing and inflating their innocence or righteousness.

"Two men went up to the temple to pray, one a Pharisee and the other a tax collector" (Luke 18:10). The tax collector, a secular and dishonest grafter, stands a great distance from the altar, smites his breast, and with downcast eyes confesses, "I am a sinner. God, be merciful to me." The Pharisee, a very religious man, also stands apart from the crowd. His belief in himself as a righteous person fills him with contempt for those who do not match his goodness. "God, I thank you that I am not like other people. I am not a thief, a rogue, an adulterer, or even like this tax collector." To sharpen the contrast, the Pharisee highlights his deeds of supererogation: "I fast twice a week. I give a tenth of all my income" (Luke 18:12).

The Pharisee is the epitome of self-justification. He goes to the temple to pray, supposedly to stand humbly before God, and instead he flaunts his righteousness and stands in contempt of his fellow human beings. His justification of himself is two-sided.

Negatively, it is an extended endeavor to deny his guilt. While the tax collector confesses, "I am a sinner" and pleads "God be merciful to me," the Pharisee would have none of it. He is convinced that he is guiltless and godly, and he prides himself in not being like other people. In actual fact, he is probably more like the people he condemns than he would care to admit, because that admission would deflate his façade of goodness.

With a little imagination, we can find the Pharisee guilty of all three forms of guilt. First, the Pharisee alludes to transgression guilt, but he ignores the many ways in which he disobeys the law and selects two ways in which he apparently keeps the law. He fasts and he tithes. Given his attitude of self-righteousness, we wonder if his deeds are more show than genuine acts of obedience. He may fulfill the letter of the law (its legalistic requirements) but fail to fulfill the spirit of the law (to love God with his whole heart and to love the neighbor as himself). The answer seems obvious from the Pharisee's behavior.

Second, the Pharisee fails to acknowledge the second form of guilt, the way in which he negates life in himself and in others. In his haste to put people down, he sees people as he wants to see them, as immoral and unfaithful creatures who are far from being as obedient and good as he is. Furthermore, his arrogance precludes any possibility of genuine dialogue with the other person. He reduces the other person to someone who at best does not measure up and who at worst is only worthy of disrespect and contempt. In any conversation with another person, he would be more monological than dialogical, more concerned to tell his story and to voice his demands than to hear, and to give credence to, the other person. This in itself is a violation of the person, if not by overt desecration then by reducing the other person to an impersonal "It."

Third, the Pharisee has no sense of ultimate guilt. Instead of acknowledging his alienation from God, he believes that he is on God's side and is busy doing God's will— praying, fasting, and doing other godly deeds. He stands in stark contrast to the tax collector, who is mindful of his sin against God and who is aware of his need for forgiveness. "I am a sinner. God, be merciful to me."

Positively, self-justification is a concerted effort to parade one's righteousness. The Pharisee's contempt was based on his firm and egocentric conviction that he was unimpeachable before God and man.

Self-righteousness is self-serving, and it tends to establish its case by citing the individual's works. The justification of what the self does or fails to do is not an innocent and inconsequential activity. It goes to the heart of human evil, not only in our relationship with God but also in our relationship with each other. In its most common form, it is manifest in the person who feels attacked and becomes defensive. The person tries to explain away a mistake or a fault in an attempt to keep his "gleaming" image untarnished. In its most blatant form, it is a destructive desecration of the other person. The desecration may be non-physical as well as physical, for an unkind word, made jagged by contempt, can be as destructive as any physical assault.

Self-justification need not be a clamorous act of arrogance, but persons who engage in it seem confident of their absolute goodness. Underneath the façade, other things may be going on. They may think of themselves as victims, which in their mind only proves the rightness of their cause and the need to be aggressive. Also, they may suffer from an underlying sense of inadequacy and low self-esteem. If the self-justified person had a solid sense of his or her worth-whileness, there would be no need for justification. Thus self-doubt is often not extraneous to pride but a source of it. Pride and self-doubt are two sides of the same coin, the one feeding into the other.

What shows in all of this is self-justification, even self-aggrandizement. Theologically, we are talking about hubris, the elevation of the self above the God who created it. "In being untrue to God, [human beings] are even more profoundly untrue to themselves and so are shattered upon a rock of self-contradiction."[2] The self gets caught in the feverish attempt to make itself good and acceptable, even as it labors against the violence it has done to itself. The violence, then, is often projected onto others who become the innocent victims of the person's righteous indignation.

The Pharisee left the temple as he came—pretentious and unforgiven. He may have felt good for displaying his righteousness and for looking down on the poor tax collector, but in fact he was still as deceived and as troubled as he was when he came. Basking in his own righteousness did not put him on the right road to fulfillment. Neither was he reconciled to God. "I tell you, the [tax collector] went down to his house justified rather than the [Pharisee]" (Luke 18:14). What the Pharisee lacked was humility or, in Paul's terms, "love in a spirit of gentleness" (1 Cor 4:21). Paul is emphasizing both a concern for others rather than the self and a spirit of meekness that eschews power and

2. Jungel, *Death*, 65.

prestige. What the Pharisee could have experienced was a genuine sense of peace with God and a healing sense of harmony with himself and others. But he was too arrogant, too impressed with himself to walk humbly with God or any other person.

Seven

Inside Shame

Shame is an all-consuming and devastating experience. It appears without warning, imprisons without mercy, and immobilizes without remorse.

It happened in a dormitory room. Nine-year-old Philip is in his cubicle and gets into bed. He pulls the blanket over himself, so his club-foot could not be seen. One of his classmates, a bully, sticks his head into Philip's cubicle and asks to see his foot. Philip refuses. The bully, and a boy in the next cubicle, try to pull the blanket off of Philip, but to no avail. The bully grabs Philip's arm and begins to turn it. Philip gasps and pleads for the boy to stop, but the bully only repeats his order. Philip tightens his grip on the blanket. The bully gives Philip's arm another wrench. The pain becomes unbearable, and Philip in desperation puts out his foot. The boys look at the foot and react with disgust.

After the boys return to their own cubicles, Philip sobs. He sinks his teeth into the pillow, hoping that his crying cannot be heard. "He was not crying for the pain they had caused him, nor for the humiliation he had suffered when they looked at his foot, but with rage at himself because, unable to stand the torture, he had put out his foot of his own accord."[1]

The Dynamics of Shame

Philip is not experiencing guilt for a misdeed. He is experiencing shame for a failure. The failure is that he did not live up to his own expectations of himself. He thought he was strong but instead found that he was weak. His weakness was incongruous with his image of himself and with the person he hoped to be. He judged himself harshly and reacted to the exposure with rage at himself and with a nagging sense of inadequacy. In a word, Philip was immersed in shame. In Sigmund Freud's terms, he did not measure up to his ego ideal, to his conception of what he should be or do.

Our analysis indicates that shame is not a one-dimensional reality. On the contrary, it is a whole complex of events bearing directly on our standing with ourselves and with the world. The basic feeling in shame is one of disgrace or of being degraded. We suffer diminished stature in our own eyes, if not in the eyes of other people. The disgrace comes because an unacceptable part of us has been exposed, often suddenly and unexpectedly. The exposed part is incongruous with our perception of ourselves or with the self we would like to be. The disgrace can also come because what we took for granted about ourselves or the world did not turn out to be true, and we felt foolish and shamed. The trigger that sets off shame need not be momentous. It can

1. Maugham, *Of Human Bondage*, 47.

be as simple as a social custom we failed to honor or a local expectation we failed to respect. Whatever the trigger, our failure resonates in our soul and diminishes our stature in a world of otherwise OK people.

Shame, like anxiety, attacks the foundation of the self. Unlike anxiety, it is not an attack on what makes us feel secure, but it is an attack on our identity, on who we are or, in the case of Philip, on who we think we should be. In any case, we find it difficult, if not impossible, to stand outside the experience of shame with any sense of confidence. Shame is made possible by our ability to transcend ourselves, but once we are immersed in it, it is difficult to extricate ourselves from it.

Since shame is a matter of identity, who we are in any one instance can bring on shame faster than what we do. Still, shame can be cued off by our doing or by our being, but the basic cause of any attack is our inability to accept whatever has been exposed.

Persons with low self-esteem are more likely to be plunged into shame than persons with a healthier opinion of themselves. By the same token, persons with big egos (or strong defenses) seldom, if ever, seem to manifest shame, not even when their action warrants it. They seem to be shameless—a reaction that seems to signal a lack of integrity and a questionable identity.

Once we experience shame, we can develop a fear of its recurrence. Our fear can bring on shame even though we are not doing or being anything that is shameful. We can also develop defenses against shame, e.g., we can avoid situations that embarrass us or we can avoid people who humiliate us.

We can feel shame for another person, but it means that the other person is doing or being something that would make us very uncomfortable with ourselves. We may find ourselves distancing, or even disowning, the other person lest we be drawn into shame, either the other person's shame or our own. So shame is essentially disjunctive. It raises a question about our being acceptable, it leaves us with an experience that is difficult to articulate and share, and it lingers in our mind as an unbridgeable breach in our relationships with other people.

Shame is inherent in every guilt and guilt is inherent in every shame. A sense of guilt is the feeling that by thought, word, or deed we have been involved in wrongdoing. Potentially, a sense of shame is right below the surface. If our wrongdoing says something about us as a person, we might feel shame, that is, we might feel exposed to, and rejected by, ourselves if not by others. For example, if we go through a stop sign, we experience or should experience guilt. We have transgressed the law and we feel guilty in the presence of the policeman who stopped us. While we are feeling guilty, we notice that there are bystanders who witnessed our deed and are amused by our plight. A sense of guilt may turn into a sense of shame. Not only have we disobeyed a law, but that disobedience represents a significant blemish on our law-abiding image of ourselves. A transgression has turned into a perceived failure.

The reverse can also be true. Shame can turn into guilt, though that may be less evident. Having gone through the stop sign, we may be shamed by the offense, that is, we may feel exposed and unacceptable. In order to ease the discomfort, we may turn the shame into a guilt by reducing the incident to a mere and inconsequential breaking of the law. In fact, we can, and maybe often do, avoid shame by this means. We make a potentially shameful act into a mere disobedience and thus avoid the embarrassment of a flushed face. We sometimes go further. In our own minds, we rationalize, or even deny, that we committed the offense at all and thus cancel out both guilt and shame.

The Function of Shame

As we have seen, shame functions in relation to our expectations of ourselves. Actually, it functions in other ways too, e.g. we may be shamed when we pretend to be somebody we're not or when we tell an off-color joke in mixed company. But for the moment we want to focus on shame as a barometer of how we are doing in relation to our ideals.

Shame serves our ideals well, but what it does not do is to evaluate the reasonableness or the worthwhileness of our ideals. For example, Philip felt shame for not being strong in the midst of pain, but shame did not say how realistic or how valuable that expectation was. It simply judged Philip for his failure.

Shame, like unhealthy guilt feelings, can serve a questionable purpose. Just as a sense of guilt can protect and enhance a faulty life-style (character), so a sense of shame can serve our unrealistic (and unhealthy) expectations. It makes no distinction between realistic and unrealistic expectations; it simply fills us with a sense of disgrace when we do not fulfill or live up to our expectations (ego ideal).

Karen Horney has said that under adverse circumstances we try to actualize an idealized image of ourselves that strives to achieve an absolute and insatiable perfection. In a word, we live by what we want to be instead of by what we really are. Ernest Becker comes at the situation from a different direction but arrives at a similar conclusion. He maintains that given the mortal threat of our finite existence, we strive to be of enduring value, of immortal significance.[2] Theology sounds a similar note. When we dealt with ultimate guilt, we were confronted with our self-centeredness. Kierkegaard and other theologians maintain that we have turned from God in unbelief in order to be the source of our own fulfillment. Instead of being centered in the source of life, we have made ourselves the center.

All of these witnesses indicate that our expectations can be unrealistic if not grandiose. A sense of shame does not critique these strivings but simply sounds an alarm when we fail to measure up to them. In this sense, shame is not a monitor of authentic aspirations but merely a sign of failure. To turn the tables on shame we could say that shame can be shameless in its failure to critique our expectations.

Our Reaction to Shame

The story of Adam and Eve (Gen 3:1–19) introduces our next concern about shame: What is our reaction to being shamed? How do we handle it? When Adam and Eve ate of the fruit of the tree, they incurred guilt because they disobeyed God's command not to eat of the tree. Their eyes were opened by their transgression, and they knew that they had crossed over into forbidden territory. Their guilt turned into shame when they heard God walking in the

2. Becker, *The Denial of Death*, 5.

garden. They hid themselves among the trees before God even asked, "Where are you?" Adam confessed, "I heard the sound of you in the garden, and I was afraid, because I was naked and I hid myself." The prospect of being seen by God for who they were drove Adam and Eve into hiding. They then tried to cover their shame by fig leaves.

Adam and Eve point to one of our first responses to shame, to being exposed. We hide from ourselves, from those who can see us, and from the presence of God. We run for cover in order to conceal our nakedness, that is, the truth that has been exposed. And we often engage in a second maneuver. When Adam was asked if he had "eaten from the tree," he quickly responded, "The woman whom you gave to be with me, she gave me fruit from the tree, and I ate." And the woman, in turn, when she was in the spotlight, said, "The serpent tricked me, and I ate." Both Adam and Eve shift the blame to someone else, and after the shift they are able to confess, "I did it," which partly takes responsibility for what they did and partly portrays them as passive victims. In addition, Adam and Eve make a clever move. In their conversation with God, they shift the focus from shame to guilt, from being exposed as persons who seek knowledge and immortality in order to be like God to being well-intentioned neonates who ate from the tree.

In offering this analysis of Adam and Eve, I do not pretend to be doing a disciplined exegesis of the text, but I think I have lifted out the experiential wisdom in the story as it relates to our response to shame. What we do not learn from the story is Adam and Eve's inner struggle with shame. My own experience may throw some light on it. As a teenager and young adult, I experienced shame as a dreadful and debilitating experience that I tried to avoid at all costs. It proceeded from low self-esteem, which also tended to increase and empower it. My world became as small and as tightly controlled as I could make it, partly because shame gave me no clue as to why it was occurring. Of course, I could give reasons and certainly I could think of things I had done that might invite it, but if they were true my sense of shame was really a sense of guilt that should have been absolved by the church's declaration of forgiveness.

People, even friends, did not help me to live with shame. For some reason, they thought that blushing was cute, and so they made an issue of it every time I blushed. That only increased my sense of isolation and powerlessness and confirmed my impression that people can be cruel.

Parents, too, played a part in my shame. As Helen Merrell Lynd says, "The overall quality of shame involves the whole life of a person, . . .[and that includes] parents who have created and nurtured [us]."[3] My parents thought humility was a prized virtue, and they were diligent in making sure that I did not think of himself more highly than I should. Somehow I ended up with low self-esteem and was an easy target for shame when I felt that I did not measure up. Not only did I feel shame for myself but also I felt shame for my parents who, in my eyes, fell short of the community's standards. Shame became a way of life in our family, not as an explicit dynamic but as an implicit threat if we did not "aim high" and "achieve the best."

On a Sunday visit to one of my aunts, I saw finger nail clippers for the first time in my life. I thought it was extra neat and stuck it in my pocket. A few days later my mother,

3. Helen Merrell Lynd, *On Shame and the Search for Identity*, 56.

with clippers in hand, confronted me. I squirmed and said I was sorry, but that was not enough. The next Sunday I had to stand before relatives, admit to my aunt that I had taken her clippers, and return the darn thing to her. My aunt was gracious (I think she had been forewarned), but no kindness could erase the pain I felt. "Aim high" but in the right direction; "do your best" but not by taking something that doesn't belong to you.

Shame, then, elicits from us a complex reaction—so complex that we have only touched its surface. In actuality, there are many different degrees of shame, ranging from a slight embarrassment to a total incapacitation of the self. I have chosen to focus on some of its more traumatic dimensions, because those dimensions need our attention. What I haven't done is to describe shame's positive potential. After all, shame does have redeeming value, even though its potential value is also its devastating power. It throws a penetrating and unforgiving light on the state of our being, both in relation to ourselves and in relation to the world around us. Shame does not pick on a little corner of our existence but goes straight to the center and illuminates who we are and how we have failed to meet expectations. It does not dwell on obvious truths about ourselves but exposes truths that we have never known or long forgotten. Finally, it witnesses to the great interconnectedness of life. It is not limited to our relationship with ourselves, but it is connected with, and has implications for, our relationships in all other areas of life. My shame, for example, may have been rooted in my relationship with parents, but it affected my relationship with siblings, with peers, with relatives, with school personnel, with church, and with God. Shame even said something to me about life itself—how I fit into it and what its possible meaning and purpose was for me.

Shame is not for the weak of mind or heart. It has been said that, unlike guilt, shame comes with no sense of condemnation. My experience indicates that the experience itself can be easily seen as a condemnation. When I felt shamed, I felt judged and rejected and, in turn, I rejected myself. At best, shame seems to serve a punitive function on the way to fulfillment. It is a deeper, more holistic disclosure of the self than a sense of guilt is and therefore it can immobilize the self in ways that guilt does not. Unfortunately, shame overkills and thus it is often more debilitating than it is facilitating. Nevertheless, if we have the courage to survive its onslaught and can take seriously its critique of the self, it can result in basic and decisive changes in the self. In the meantime, shame may have to be content with small victories like making a thief of nail clippers into a law-abiding citizen.

Eight

Guilt Feelings
A Road to Fulfillment

I have made a startling discovery in my old age. I thought that guilt was not for old people, but at eighty-one I find that at times I look back on my younger years and feel great remorse. When I think of some of the things I have done in my life or some of the ways in which I have used people, I am filled with regret. While I do not feel condemned outrightly by my past deeds, I do feel very sorry for my thoughtless and selfish actions. So I find that guilt lingers in my consciousness and sometimes casts a troubling shadow on my older years.

My experience raises a question about the positive role of guilt in our journey through life. To paraphrase the title of a pastoral book on guilt: Is guilt a curse or a blessing? Or more pointedly: Under what circumstances does guilt guide us toward authentic fulfillment? I think of two approaches to the question, but they do not speak directly to

the role of guilt in fulfillment. They maintain that fulfillment is achieved apart from a direct struggle with guilt.

In its more optimistic form, existentialism maintains
that human fulfillment is a product of our own making. We
have been given the freedom to choose, and thus we can
take destiny into our own hands and shape our lives according to our best intentions. But there are obstacles along the
way. There is the inevitability of anxiety, guilt, and death,
but if we faced these challenges head-on, they become a
vital part of our becoming. There is also the threat of mean-
inglessness, but we have the power to choose new meanings
and the ability to pursue new directions. Fulfillment, then,
is within our reach if we live life wisely and courageously.

To humanistic psychologists, fulfillment is to become
"all we can be." It is to actualize what Carl Rogers calls the
real self, that is, to follow our own inherent tendency to
make decisions and to choose paths that are fulfilling for
us. We can become "fully functioning" persons: We can
perceive reality accurately, including the reality that we are.
We can live in the present instead of repeating the past or
living in the future. We can trust our own valuing process
instead of living by the values and demands of others. We
are free to make choices and to take responsibility for those
choices. And we can live creatively by contributing to the
actualization of others and by making the world a better
place to live. Fulfillment, then, is within our grasp if we follow the inherent wisdom of our original nature.

Instances of Guilt

There is value in both existentialism and in humanistic psychology, but I want to be more direct and more concrete about the role of guilt and guilt feelings by dealing with an extended and concrete instance of both of them. Khaled Hosseini's novel *The Kite Runner* comes to mind. It is a richly moving story, told with the skill of a real literary artist and filled with the wisdom of a keen observer of the human condition. After retelling a part of the story, I will use it for my own purposes, but in no way should that be taken as a critique of the author's masterful novel.

In *The Kite Runner*, Amir and Hassan are close and loyal friends. They were raised virtually in the same family—Amir was the son of an influential and wealthy businessman named Baba; Hassan was the son of Ali, a servant in Baba's household. They played together as equals, though at night Amir went to his father's mansion and Hassan went to the servant's mud house. The two boys were inseparable and shared the fun of childhood pranks. When they got into trouble, Hassan always protected Amir and never denied any of his wishes, if Amir was persistent.

Amir spent his childhood years trying to get his father Baba's approval. Baba was an assertive, demanding person who did not take to Amir's more laid-back ways. Every year Amir entered a kite flying tournament, hoping to emerge as the winner. With Hassan as his first-rate kite runner, Amir stood a good chance of winning the tournament. Still, victory escaped him, which only proved Baba's impression that his son did not have what it takes to be a man.

On a beautiful, blue sky day, when Amir was twelve years old, he was persuaded by Hassan to enter the kite tournament again. After many hours of competition, Amir's kite and a blue kite were the only ones still in the air. By a clever maneuver, Amir cut the string of the blue kite, sending it into a wild spin. Hassan volunteered to run after the blue kite and retrieve it in order to confirm Amir's victory.

Hassan took off through the streets, knowing intuitively where the kite might return to the ground. When Hassan did not come back as expected, Amir became worried and searched up and down the streets to find Hassan. Amir followed the sound of voices coming from an alley, and as he rounded the corner he saw the blue kite sitting on "piles of scrap and rubble."[1] His eyes moved to Hassan who was standing "at the blind end of the alley," imprisoned by three boys who had been humiliated by Hassan in a recent encounter. Amir watched from a hidden vantage point as the third boy, Assef, demanded that Hassan hand over the blue kite, robbing Amir of his trophy and of his chance to impress Baba. Hassan refused, saying that it belonged to Amir. Assef grew impatient and had his two companions subdue Hassan while he positioned himself behind Hassan and raped him.

As Amir watched, he knew there was an opportune time to intervene on Hassan's behalf. He could emerge from his hiding place and stand with Hassan as Hassan had done for him many times. But he would have to endure (take) whatever Assef and his two friends decided to dish out. He thought for a moment and then decided to run. He retreated to a safe place and waited until the three boys left

1. Hosseini, *The Kite Runner*, 71.

the alley. He retraced his steps until he met Hassan. Hassan
"swayed on his feet" but did not collapse. He handed Amir
the blue kite and "limped away."[2]

In the Wake of Guilt

The force of what Amir had done hit him immediately and
was reinforced by Hassan's quiet anguish. Amir could admit
to himself that he was afraid of what Assef might do to him.
He did not want to get hurt. He even said to himself that
maybe his friend Hassan was the price he had to pay to have
the blue kite and to be able to take it home to Baba.

All of these thoughts did not stop the torture of guilt
or the piercing sense of having betrayed Hassan. He could
have stood with Hassan, but instead he chose to run. He
was devastated, knowing that he had participated in diminishing or even destroying a friend's life.

Amir's guilt was a wrenching experience for Amir and
for everyone whose life was touched by Amir. Amir's guilt
was not an openly-admitted fact. It may have caused less
damage if Amir had had the courage and honesty to confess
what he had done, but instead he tried to hide it and to live
with the pretense.

Amir suspected that Hassan knew that he had been
betrayed and that he had even told his father Ali about the
betrayal. And Baba suspected that there was something
radically wrong between Amir and Hassan when Amir
asked his father if he ever thought about getting "new
servants." Baba's response was decisive: "Hassan's not going anywhere, do you understand?" Without pursuing the

2. Ibid., 78.

matter further, Baba suggested that if there was something going on between Amir and Hassan, Amir should be man enough to deal with it.[3]

Amir's guilt ripped him and all of his relationships apart. He saw himself as a coward. At another time, he describes himself as a monster who dragged Hassan to the bottom of a murky lake. At the mere mention of Hassan's name, Amir felt a pair of steel hands close around his windpipe.

Guilt certainly tore Amir's relationship with Hassan apart. It pulled it up by the roots and threw it on a rubbish pile. Both Amir and Hassan tried to recover their closeness, but there was only the charred ashes of what once was. Amir got to a point where he could not stand Hassan's kindness toward him. One day the two of them were picking fruit from a pomegranate tree when Amir retrieved a pomegranate that had fallen to the ground. "What would you do if I hit you with this?" Amir asked. Hassan gave no response. Amir flung the fruit at Hassan, hitting him in the chest. "Hit me back," Amir demanded. When Hassan did not return the attack, Amir pelted Hassan with more pomegranates, trying to provoke Hassan into attacking him. But Hassan remained unshaken, like an unblemished lamb, and Amir was stuck with the death-pangs of guilt. He broke down and sobbed.

Amir's relationship with Hassan and his father Ali deteriorated until Ali announced that they could no longer live and work at Baba's place. Baba was confused and mortified but could not talk Ali out of leaving. Amir watched as Baba drove Ali and Hassan off the grounds,

3. Ibid., 89.

and he realized "that the life [he] had known since [he'd] been born was over."[4]

In fairness to Amir we have to grant that he faced a tough moral and psychological decision—to save himself from Assef's fury or to stand up for his friend Hassan and suffer the consequences. We can understand why he chose to avoid Assef's lawlessness, but the price he paid was immense. His unconfessed guilt drove him down a jagged path. Amir's guilt condemned him as a coward or later as a monster or later still as gutless. Loaded with an intolerable sense of guilt, Amir sought to redeem himself. He pelted Hassan with pomegranates, turning his body into a gruesome display of red juice and pulp. Hassan did not strike back,[5] and Amir was left wrung out and unpunished. He lived with a tortured conscience for years until Rahim Khan, Baba's friend and business partner, offered him "a way to end the cycle of [lies and betrayals], a way to be good again."[6]

The path was straightforward but full of sacrifice. Amir was to leave his wife and family in California and return to his native town of Kabul in Afghanistan on a rescue mission. Rahim told him that Hassan had been killed by the Taliban but that Hassan had left a son named Sohrab, who as an orphan was "wasting away." Rahim asked Amir to go and bring Sohrab home with him.

Amir resisted at first but soon accepted the mission and went to great lengths to atone for his betrayal of Hassan. In Kabul, he met obstacle after obstacle: He had to

4. Ibid., 108.
5. Ibid., 92–93.
6. Ibid., 226.

gain Sohrab's release from the orphanage, he had to fight immigration laws and adoption agency policies, and he had to win Sohrab's trust because Sohrab had been deeply wounded by the invasive seductions of Assef and other men. He was just beginning to win that trust when he was forced to go back on his promise to Sohrab to never put him in an orphanage again. Sohrab withdrew into himself and trusted no one. When Amir and Sohrab finally got home to California, Sohrab was a frustration more than an atonement. He did not speak to Amir and his wife for months. Amir's attempt to atone for his betrayal of Hassan was ambiguous at best.

Ironically, what helped Amir work through his guilt more than anything else was an encounter with Assef, who was now a member of the Taliban and the supervisor over Sohrab. When Amir asked to take Sohrab out of the orphanage, Assef challenged him to a fight and brutalized him with stainless-steel brass knuckles. Amir was near death, but in the midst of it he felt strangely at peace. "My body was broken—just how badly I wouldn't find out until later—but I felt healed. Healed at last."[7] The violence he did not take from Assef years earlier when he could have stood with Hassan now becomes the instrument of his healing.

What if?

We have sketched the trajectory of Amir's unconfessed guilt. It has led through a minefield of pretenses and failed endeavors. But it serves as a backdrop for what might have

---

7. Ibid., 289.

happened if Amir had been open about his betrayal. What does guilt achieve when it functions properly?

When Amir met Hassan coming from the alley, he had a second chance to be open and honest with Hassan. Instead of concealing his betrayal, he could have revealed his guilt. Amir and Hassan's long-standing relationship could have withstood the confession, especially since Hassan had a tendency to protect Amir. The confession may have introduced a crisis into the relationship that would have to be worked through, but it could have become an occasion for growth and renewal, not just in Amir and Hassan's relationship but in Amir's relationship with himself and other people. Reconstructing the story along those lines discloses the potentially positive function of guilt feelings.

If Amir had met Hassan with the confession, "I'm sorry. I saw what was happening, but I was afraid," Hassan could have reacted in a number of different ways. He could have turned on Amir, berating him for his lack of courage. Or he could have simply fallen into Amir's arms and experienced a momentary reprieve. Or again he could have accepted Amir's confession and drawn strength and support from his friend. Actually, Hassan's response would probably have been a mixture of all three reactions, but Amir would have been available to Hassan as he struggled with the physical and psychological trauma of being raped. What Hassan needed at that point was someone to help him, a friend who he could trust and lean on in his hour of pain and humiliation. He needed this support and had a right to expect it from a friend, even if Hassan had been bitter and resentful toward him.

As for Amir, if he had admitted his failure he would have thought of himself in a more positive light. Instead of feeling like a coward, he would have seen himself as at least a semi-brave person who finally got it right. The benefit to Amir would have gone beyond a positive perception of himself. Guilt feelings are a call to responsibility, both a call to take responsibility for what we have done or not done and a call to be responsible to the person who needs our help. Confession would have helped Amir to be responsible in both senses. He would have been honest about his failure to act and maybe about his reason for not acting. In this sense, he would have been more truthful and more trustworthy in his relationship with Hassan. He would have "rung true" rather than being deceptive. He would also have been more responsive to Hassan. Hassan's needs, both physical and psychological, were great as he came out of the alley. Amir was so busy hiding his guilt that he was insensitive to Hassan. Confession of guilt would have freed and empowered Amir to see some of Hassan's needs and to respond to them in a more direct and, hopefully, a more fitting way. The relationship between the two friends would have deepened in both trust and comradeship.

It is more speculative about how Amir's confession of guilt might have influenced the relationship with his father. For years, Baba pressed Amir to be more assertive and manly. If Amir had told him of his betrayal of Hassan, Baba's reaction may have been violent, especially since Baba had a special interest in Hassan's welfare. Baba may have been confirmed in his belief that Amir was a wimp. Then again, Baba could have reacted to Amir's confession in a positive way. He could have appreciated the courage it took for Amir to come clean, especially since he himself lived a lie that he never confessed (or acknowledged). Besides, with Baba's special interest in Hassan, Baba may have been pleased that Amir showed respect and concern for Hassan. In either case, if Amir had confessed, he would have removed one of the lies that stood between father and son (Amir and Baba).

What would Amir's confession have done for the relationship between Baba and his friend Ali? We know what his pretense did to the relationship. It tore it asunder, because Ali and Hassan got to a point where they could no longer live and work in Baba's household. If Amir had been honest with Ali, Ali may have been upset with Amir and been critical of his failure to help, but there would have been a chance for reconciliation to occur. Either Amir or Ali could have taken the initiative to bridge the gap—Amir by apologizing for his lack of courage and Ali by acknowledging the tough decision that Amir faced. But what Amir's confession would have really accomplished was to call him back from the thoughtless and self-serving comment that Hassan was only a Hazara and that maybe he was the price that Amir had to pay to impress Baba with the kite. In admitting his guilt, Amir would be respecting Hassan as a person, as a fellow human being who was worthy of honesty and concern.

Amir's hidden and unredeemed guilt played itself out in his marital relationship too. When Amir and his wife were considering whether to adopt a child or not, Amir was against the possibility, because he felt unworthy of it. "Perhaps something, someone, somewhere had decided to deny me fatherhood for the things I had done. Maybe this was my punishment, and perhaps justly so."[8]

Amir reacted differently when Rahim Khan offered him a way to be good again. He accepted the opportunity, the challenge to go back to Afghanistan and rescue Hassan's son Sohrab. Once in Afghanistan with Sohrab, Amir saw first hand what being raped might have done to his friend Hassan. Sohrab was untouchable, flinching at any sign of physical contact. He was withdrawn and depressed, imprisoned in his own little world. There were moments when Sohrab was more available, but any indication of closeness sent Sohrab back into his gated existence.

Amir's attempt "to be good again" turned out to be an ambivalent experience at best. In fact, it may have increased Amir's sense of guilt and reloaded his sense of impending judgment. He failed in ways that he did not want to fail. He did not succeed in drawing Sohrab out but instead drove him into greater solitude when he explained to Sohrab that he may have to go back into an orphanage. He attempted to be open and trustworthy, but he never convinced Sohrab that he could be trusted. He could easily feel that he let Sohrab down just as much earlier he had let Hassan down. His mission "to be good again" was never good enough to cancel out his own sense of indebtedness to Hassan or to overcome Sohrab's sense of being violated. And at the end of the story, Amir consoles himself with the dim hope that his relationship with Sohrab may improve someday.

We have used the story of Amir to disclose the potentially positive function of guilt when we are courageous enough to admit it. The confession of guilt offers no

8. Hosseini, *The Kite Runner*, 188.

automatic guarantees. The person we have offended may or may not think kindly of our betrayal. The relationships we have distorted and tarnished may not be able to withstand our wrongdoing. The damage we have done to ourselves may or may not be reparable. But the honest admission of guilt, to ourselves if not to others, has certain benefits. The constant attempt to decide who knows what and who doesn't know is not an issue. The endless need to live a lie and keep up the pretense is not necessary. And the feverish attempt to make ourselves good does not haunt our days or trouble our nights. We are more available to people, and people, in turn, are more responsive to us. They can grant, or at least can identify with, our human imperfections and faulty decisions. They can appreciate our honesty and resonate with our remorse. They tend to stop judging us and begin to stand with us. If our guilt feelings prompt us to admit and confess our guilt, they have served a potentially positive function in our search for fulfillment. They have opened the way to reconciliation and deeper growth.

Conclusion

As we have seen, the potential benefits of guilt feelings are activated in and through the confession of guilt. We need to add a further word about "confessing our guilt." We have implied that confession should be "a public declaration" or at least an explicit acknowledgment of guilt to the person whom we have offended. The case of Hester Prynne reinforces this notion, since Hester's guilt was available for all to see when she appeared on the public scaffold and as she wore the scarlet letter. O. Hobart Mowrer, in chapter

1, reinforces a similar thought when he maintains that in order to be free of our "tangible social misdeeds," we must face the truth and confess the foul deed to people whose opinion matters to us. Mowrer is asking for acknowledgment and honesty instead of secrecy and denial. He is also right in saying that guilt requires of us a certain payment and, if possible, some form of restitution.

But Mowrer's understanding of confession is limited. It is act-oriented, involving a particular social misdeed or a series of social misdeeds instead of giving any recognition to negation guilt and ultimate guilt. It is a public *mea culpa*, involving the person or persons we have offended. And it tends to be more punitive (the price we have to pay) than it is a cleansing (a regretful recognition of what we have done or been). While confession may or may not include any or all of these elements, for us it is basically and primarily an attitude, an inward disposition of truthfully facing and honestly owning up to our guilt. It acknowledges not just what we have done (our doing) but the self-centered pursuit of our wants and wishes. It can be a public admission of guilt, but it can also be a deeply and inward acknowledgment of our wrongdoing. And it can be punitive, but more so it is an admission (an acknowledgment) of the heart, a disposition of our very being. Confession is similar to the Christian understanding of repentance, not just an outward regret but an inward turning, a reorientation of our lives. Anything less than this falls short of a confession that frees us.

Confession and restitution, however noble, are not the end of our struggle with guilt and guilt feelings. Amir's story reminds us that we never achieve full or final fulfillment. There is always the need for something more, something that addresses our persistent failures and faulty fulfillments. In the next chapter, we take that needed step.

Nine

The Cost of Guilt and the Gift of God

As we have seen, guilt is costly. It exacts a price, sometimes a heavy price, from us in our personal and interpersonal lives.

In the first place, guilt is costly to the persons who have been hurt or diminished by our wrongdoing, examples from previous chapters come to mind. Hester Prynne committed adultery in a puritanical New England community, and her guilt extracted a price from everyone who was related to her. Chillingworth, Hester's husband, felt betrayed and turned into a vengeful caricature of himself. Pearl, Hester's "fatherless" child, was born an outcast and with Hester lived in a "circle of seclusion" apart from the community. And Dimmesdale, the pastor, though not under public scrutiny for years, paid the price for his adultery by losing his health and living with a sense of hypocrisy. In a wider sense, the community itself felt that its image had been diminished or tarnished by having one of its members engage in unseemly behavior. As a show of disapproval, those in charge put Hester on public display.

Amir's unconfessed guilt provides us with another instance of the price paid by people, often innocent people, who are hurt by our wrongdoing. Hassan, Amir's friend, paid a hefty price by being violated and humiliated. Ali, Hassan's father, sacrificed the security of his job and the benevolent friendship of Baba, his employer. And Baba lost Amir to Amir's preoccupation with his betrayal of Hassan.

In the second place, guilt is costly to the person who does what is wrong or fails to do what is right. Amir was tortured by his failure to stand by Hassan, and later in life he was driven to try to redeem himself by leaving his home and returning to Afghanistan to rescue Hassan's son Sohrab. Hester, too, paid a horrible and life-long price, for a single act of adultery. And Andy, the rising basketball star who never forgave himself for his buddy's death, paid with his life.

In all these instances the more guilt is denied, the more costly it becomes. That is certainly true in the case of Kafka's K. who, when he was asked directly if he was without guilt, said, "Yes." And then he savored the pleasure more by adding, "I am totally innocent."[1] Meanwhile, K. was living a shallow life of alienation and guilt and suffered the destructive consequences. In the case of Amir and Andy, it is not denial that makes guilt costly but the failure to deal with guilt. Amir knew that he was guilty, but he did nothing about it until he returned to Afghanistan. Andy, too, knew he was guilty, but he never addressed his guilt. Even when

1. Kafka, *The Trial,* 141.

he went to a psychiatrist, he tried to remain "cool" and un-involved, until it was too late.

The Cost to God

In addition to guilt being costly to self and others, guilt is also costly to God. We will use Paul and Luther's under-standing of our plight to make the point, since their whole theological stance is a story about God dealing with our sin, guilt, and restoration.

In our discussion of ultimate guilt (chapter three), we found that we are alienated from God by our failure to put our lives into God's hands. We take life into our own hands, and trust that we can be and think that we should be the source of our own sustenance and fulfillment. The fruit of our arrogance is a life of estrangement from ourselves, from others, and from God, a situation in which we constantly become our own worst enemy. We make wrong decisions, we pursue dead-ends, and we elevate our limited and finite understanding into absolute truths. Even our moments of humility and regret are tinged with an egoistic concern about what is good for us.

God could turn his back on us and leave us to our own devices. And in a way God did. Expressed metaphorically, God required Adam and Eve to pay a price for their dis-obedience. Adam obtained food to nourish his body by the sweat of his brow, and Eve bore children in the midst of pain and suffering. Both judgments deal with the continu-ation of life, and if Adam or Eve had not paid the price, it would have meant the eventual end of human life, either by lack of food or by no descendents.

We can understand God's reaction to our disobedience in at least two ways. We can see it as an act of a vindictive judge whose wrath falls on the disobedient, or we can see it as an act of a grieving father who exacted some payment from Adam and Eve for their mockery of God's parameters. I opt for the second interpretation. I think God acts as a just and loving parent who may have felt shamed by Adam and Eve's disobedient snub but who nevertheless was not vindictive but caring and conciliatory. God took our guilt and shame and death upon himself and paid the price, much as a parent might sacrifice for an errant child. There are various theories about how God did this, but the important point is that God does it in and through Christ's life and crucifixion. As Lord of both life and death, God raised Christ from the dead, which means that God was pleased with what Christ had done. The price was paid. By grasping onto Christ, we become heirs to God's grace. Grace is not a substance that is poured into us, making us righteous, but a gracious relationship that has a twofold impact on our lives. We are both empowered and pardoned by God's gift.

God Empowers Us

Have you ever been in a relationship in which you felt more alive, more confident, more focused? You may not know exactly why this particular person empowers you, but you know it is happening and you may not want it to end. That is a little like Peter, James, and John. Jesus took them up to a mountain where Jesus was transfigured before them. Elijah and Moses were also there. Peter was inspired and did not want to lose the moment. He suggested to Jesus that they build three dwellings and stay on the mountain. Jesus resisted Peter's suggestion, and when Jesus descended the mountain he extended his ministry by healing a boy who was a victim of a dumb spirit.

God's grace comes as a twofold empowerment. We have the power to move beyond the ravages of guilt and shame, and we have the power to move toward the destiny of genuine fulfillment. Fulfillment is no longer the autonomous actualization of Carl Rogers's real self or the strengthening of our innate good nature. It becomes a new possibility and can be understood in a number of different ways. First, we can understand it within the framework of our own paradoxical nature. Theologians like Soren Kierkegaard and Reinhold Niebuhr point out that we are both finite and infinite creatures. On the one hand, we are mortal and are bound by definite limitations of time and space. Like all other animals, we cannot escape the vicissitudes of our existence. On the other hand, we are transcendent beings. We can stand above our immediate circumstances and even above ourselves and live in a fabricated world of our own making. We can make our lives—and even our deaths—objects of surveillance. So we are a paradox, we are like "the grass of the field" and yet we are created "a little lower than the angels."

Our task—both our immediate and long-term task—is to find fulfillment by balancing the two poles of our existence. We are to live in a world of possibilities while we are subject to extinction at any time or, to reverse the equation, we are to live in a world of limitations and mortality while we can dream infinite dreams and can live in a "world" of our own making. The task we face is not easy, and the solution is not a given. Instead we experience anxiety from three sources—from the precariousness of our creatureliness, from the awesomeness of our possibilities, and from the conflict between the two. In order to quiet the anxiety and to live with some sense of tranquility, we tend to accentuate one side of the paradox and eliminate the other side. If we favor our creatureliness, we live in a mundane and determined world that is far removed from what and who we could be. If we favor our transcendence, we live in an awesome world of possibilities and tend to disown our limitations and mortality. Neither option leads to genuine fulfillment.

Generally, theologians agree that we tend to favor our possibilities, however scary they may be. We deny our creatureliness and accentuate our infinite nature. We attempt to be like God, to be the center of our existence. In the process, we separate ourselves from the source of life and lose the chance to become the paradoxical creatures that God created us to be.

Kierkegaard believes that we can live paradoxically only by a leap of faith in the God who created us. Anything else is a life of despair, a life of distorted or denied fulfillment. First, we can live a life that is unaware of ourselves as a self and unaware of God beyond the self. In our terms, this despair is equivalent to a total denial of ourselves and of God. Second, we can reduce the self to the finite and the immediate and live in a narrow world that shuts everything out beyond the everyday, including any recognition of God. In our terms, this despair is equivalent to living life as a mere animal or, as Lord Tennyson puts it, we become "no better than sheep or goats that nourish a blind life within the brain."[2] In the third kind of Kierkegaardian despair, we may or may not acknowledge God but in any case we refuse to accept the self that God created us to be. In our terms, this despair is equivalent to a denial of our God-given destiny and an attempt to create a fabricated self that we want to be. The antidote to all three forms of despair is to live by faith, that is, to own the self in full awareness of its paradoxical nature and to rest transparently in the God who created us.

Faith in Kierkegaard's sense is difficult to come by, but when we rest completely in God, we are empowered to live our paradoxical nature. We are creatures but more than creatures. We are finite and infinite, free and yet determined. God relates to us, and works within us, to enable us to be both a child of nature and a child of the spirit, both creature and transcendent. We are like a piece of art in progress. We are empowered to move toward what God created us to be, both in this moment and throughout our lives. We do not do that on our own. We are fulfilled, if at all, in and through a relationship with God and, secondarily, in and through a vast network of human relationships.

God's empowerment of us can be put in another framework. It involves our growth in faith. Martin Luther points the way. In his lifetime, Luther was subject to what he called *anfechtung,* to bouts of despair when he doubted that God loved him. Luther called these moments "spiritual temptations" and found that there was only one way to combat their despair. Reliance on his own resources did not work, and reassurances that "he who loves God will inherit the Kingdom of God" did not console or strengthen

2. Tennyson, *Morte d'Arthur,* line 250.

Luther. It was only steadfast faith in the promises of Christ, only total reliance "on the eternal promise of forgiveness that God had given in Christ that rescued Luther from the ravages of *anfechtung*."[3] Fulfillment, then, is growth in faith. It is not the elimination of all doubt or a greater trust in human resources, but a deeper, unconditional reliance on the promises of God, on what God does for us and to us.

God Forgives Us

God's empowerment does not prevent us from adding human error and rebellion to the mix. When we fail to be what God intended, God is merciful and offers forgiveness. Divine forgiveness is not a single zap that makes things all right nor is it an exoneration that wipes the slate clean as though we have been falsely accused. It is a whole new relationship with God. God sees our guilt and does not hold it against us. God sees our failure to live up to divine expectations and does not shame us. God sees death as the end point of our pursuit of faulty fulfillment and moves to make it a gateway to new life. God reaches out to re-establish a relationship with us and through that relationship to get us back on track. In actual fact, God's forgiveness addresses and seeks to resolve a persistent ambiguity and a final impotence on our part. It allows us to be estranged and yet related, incomplete and yet complete, distorted and yet fulfilled. This freedom to be ourselves—simultaneously guilty and forgiven—is a kind of fulfillment of its own. It is not the fulfillment of one's potential, though that may be involved, but it is the fulfillment of being accepted in spite of being

3. Gaebler, "Moments of Doubt and Growth in Faith," 92,

unacceptable. It is a fulfillment of amazing grace, of being forgiven when we deserve judgment and rejection. Or, as Tillich puts it, "Nothing greater can happen to a human being than that he is forgiven."[4]

Human Forgiveness

In forgiving us, God also empowers us to forgive. Or to paraphrase St. Paul's comment about consolation: "God forgives us, so that we may be able to forgive those who have hurt us in the same spirit in which we have been forgiven" (2 Cor 1:3). Sometimes, of course, we find it difficult, if not impossible, to forgive in spite of God's help. We are confronted by circumstances or faced with personal issues that make it hard for us to turn the other cheek. Lewis B. Smedes[5] helps us to understand some of the obstacles. We may have no desire to forgive, Smedes says, when we are attacked personally, especially by someone we trusted or when we are hurt unfairly and do not deserve it or when we suffer the consequences of being hurt for years.

Smedes highlights other reasons: To forgive a person who has hurt us, either intentionally or unintentionally, seems unfair to us, like we are letting the culprit escape scot-free. Also, to forgive a person feels like we are approving, or at least tolerating, the wrong that was done to us. Thirdly, to forgive a person feels like we are selling ourselves out, that we are too weak to stand up for our rights as a human being. And, finally, our ability to forgive a person is often impeded by our inability to understand why the

4. Tillich, *The New Being*, 2.
5. Smedes, *Forgive and Forget*.

person hurt us in the first place. What was going on in the person's mind or what did he or she intend when they hurt us? Smedes has helped us to see that there are multiple reasons why we find it difficult to forgive, and why, in some cases, we are not willing to pay the price to forgive.

John Patton offers a more psychological analysis of why human forgiveness is so difficult. In a book entitled, *"Is Human Forgiveness Possible?"* Patton maintains that our basic reaction to being a victim of wrongdoing is shame. Shame is such a total and devastating experience that we often use three basic defenses to defend ourselves against it. The defenses are rage, power, and righteousness, and each of these makes forgiveness anything but a simple possibility.

The first defense is not just anger but rage toward the person who has hurt or diminished us. Rage is a more holistic and basic emotion than anger, and it may be reinforced or intensified by the narcissistic rage that we felt as a child when we did not get the care we needed or wanted. Patton maintains that our rage, both its historic and its present forms, must be dealt with and the self must be restructured before we can think of forgiving the person who shames us.

Power is the second defense we use against shame. Patton means the power we have or can wield by forgiving or not forgiving the person who injures us. He cites the case of Tom, who wondered whether he could forgive his father for abandoning the family when Tom was around fourteen. Patton came to feel that withholding forgiveness gave Tom a great advantage in the father/son relationship. It put the father in a position of owing Tom something, and it could be used by Tom as a handy trump card "to show who is really in charge." Besides, Patton points out, Tom's failure to forgive could be used to "prove" that he is being asked to do something that is beyond his control.[6] Patton maintains that Tom would have to give up all these advantages before he would be willing to forgive his father.

Righteousness is the third term that Patton uses to describe our defense against shame. Righteousness as a biblical/theological term refers, among other things, to behavior that is appropriate to, and fulfilling of, a relationship, but Patton does not use it in that way. He refers to our self-satisfaction in being right or, in terms of shame, our compensatory feeling that over against the person who shamed us we are in the right. Patton cites Emmie who was abandoned by her husband Elmer and who hung onto the belief that she was the one who was wronged and that she had no reason to forgive Elmer. According to Patton, Emmie would have to give up this self-righteous defense before forgiveness is possible.

Over against the obsessive demands of human forgiveness stands the free gift of God's forgiveness. God forgives, not because divine forgiveness comes without a price but because God has paid the price for us. If we stay on the path of unforgiving guilt we dwell in the valley of judgment and condemnation or, just as bad, we find relief in the moralistic and arrogant assertion of our own self-righteousness. To the Christian, then, forgiveness comes as a profoundly freeing experience, releasing us from the endless and fruitless attempt to make ourselves right. We are empowered to give up our supposed righteousness and by faith to accept the fact that God accepts us in spite of our guilt and self-centeredness. Then guilt ceases to be a path to self-destruction

6. Patton, *Is Human Forgiveness Possible?*, 82.

and becomes a path to renewed life. It moves us toward who we were meant to be—the finest moral creatures on earth and the earthly agents of the God who created us. All the while God stands by to pick us up and to forgive us when we fall short of the mark.

Postscript

I have used a number of different sources to illuminate the role of guilt and guilt feelings in our search for fulfillment. Clinical and literary accounts, supplemented by conceptual ideas, have revealed a telling story of our struggle. By hearing the voice of those who suffer from guilt, I have heard again my own story.

I can identify with Amir's untimely failure to act when a friend desperately needs help. With Janet, I have experienced great disappointment with myself when my resolve to lose weight, or to achieve some other good intention, falls helpless before my darker desires. And Joseph K. in Kafka's *The Trial* is not alone in his attempt to live a shallow, unreflective life while there are great issues of identity and affirmation at stake. I recall moments when I have walked with Lady Macbeth, tormented by the desecration of a life that leaves a blemish of guilt that will not wash away, no matter how hard I try. At such moments, I look to Hester Prynne and admire her courage to live a productive life beyond the guilt and shame she bears.

The path of guilt and guilt feelings is jagged, made treacherous by our denial and self-righteousness and made passable and promising by God's grace. In any case, because the struggle is not easy, I want to add a final word or two to our search.

There is a tremendous amount of unproductive guilt in most of us. Susan Carrell speaks of it as toxic guilt and means by it excessive guilt feelings that make us feel flawed and never good enough. Harold Kushner heads in the same direction when he speaks about a guilt that makes us feel inadequate and unlovable if we do not meet the barest requirements of the law. The demand is for absolute perfection, and if we fall short the penalty is rejection and even self-condemnation.

We have to get beyond this moralistic trap. It is unfair to us. It is unfair to the basic and positive intent of guilt feelings. A sense of guilt is about our fulfillment as human beings. It is about our ability to be moral creatures who live in a world that revolves around issues of justice and love, of meaning and death. At its best, the voice of our conscience is not an external demand for acquiescence but an inner urge to be faithful to our essential self. It is the self standing over against itself, serving as a monitor of how we are proceeding on the journey to become who we were created to be.

The Christian faith adds a new and unexpected perspective to our struggle. It invites us to refocus our approach to guilt and fulfillment. It asserts that it is not what we do with guilt and guilt feelings but what God does to and for them. This reorientation comes with an ironic twist. It is in dying to ourselves that we come to life. This does not mean that we negate ourselves but that we stop making ourselves the center of life and meaning. It is in giving that we receive, for we are fulfilled not by fortifying ourselves but by building up one another.   It is in serving the neighbor in need that we discover the true meaning of life.

Both the human struggle with guilt and God's answer to guilt are legitimate and vital components of our larger encounter with guilt. The one cannot substitute for the other. Our guilt requires some response from us, which can range from denial to confession, and how we respond determines the course of our guilt. But in any case, we cannot extricate ourselves from our guilt or undo the damages that have been done to the human community. Ultimately, then, we stand before God. God alone has the authority to forgive sin and guilt and God alone is able to free us from the consequences of wrongdoing. Living in the shelter of God's compassion and forgiveness, we experience the fullness of fulfillment and turning to God we say, "Thank you for the gift. Glory be to you alone."

Bibliography

Aden, LeRoy H. *In Life and Death: The Shaping of Faith.* Minneapolis: Augsburg, 2005.

Aden, LeRoy and David G. Benner. *Counseling and the Human Predicament: A Study of Sin, Guilt, and Forgiveness.* Grand Rapids: Baker, 1989.

Aden, LeRoy and J. Harold Ellens. *The Church and Pastoral Care.* Grand Rapids: Baker, 1988.

Aden, LeRoy and Robert G. Hughes. *Preaching God's Compassion: Comforting Those Who Suffer.* Minneapolis: Fortress, 2002.

Buber, Martin. *Between Man and Man.* Translated by Ronald Gregory Smith. New York: Macmillan, 1965.

———. *I and Thou.* Translated by Walter Kaufman. New York: Scribner's, 1970.

———. *The Knowledge of Man: A Philosophy of the Interhuman.* Translated by Maurice Friedman and Ronald Gregory Smith. New York: Harper & Row, 1965.

Carrell, Susan. *Escaping Toxic Guilt: Five Proven Steps to Free Yourself from Guilt for Good.* New York: McGraw Hill, 2007.

Draper, Sharon M. *Tears of a Tiger.* New York: Simon Pulse, 1994.

Gaebler, Mary. "Moments of Doubt and Growth in Faith." Edited by LeRoy H. Aden, David G. Benner, and J. Harold Allens. *Christian Perspectives on Human Development.* Grand Rapids: Baker, 1992.

Hawthorne, Nathaniel. *The Scarlet Letter.* New York: Barnes & Noble, 2003.

Heidegger, Martin. *Being and Time.* Translated by Joan Stambaugh. Albany: University of New York Press, 1996.

Horney, Karen. *Neurosis and Human Growth: The Struggle Toward Self-Realization.* New York: Norton, 1950.

Hosseini, Khaled. *The Kite Runner.* New York: Riverhead, 2003.

Huneven, Michelle. *Blame: A Novel.* New York: Crichton, 2009.

Jungel, Eberhard. *Death: The Riddle and the Mystery.* Translated by Iain and Ute Nicol. Philadelphia: Westminster, 1974.

Kafka, Franz. *The Trial.* Translated by Willa and Edwin Muir. New York: Schocken, 1999.

Kushner, Harold S. *How Good Do We Have to Be?: A New Understanding of Guilt and Forgiveness.* New York: Little, Brown, 1996.

Lynd, Helen Merrell. *Shame and the Search for Identity.* New York: Science Editions, 1961.

Maugham, W. Somerset. *Of Human Bondage.* New York: Modern Library, 1999.

Mowrer, O. Hobart. *The Crisis in Psychiatry and Religion.* Princeton: Nostrand, 1961.

Niebuhr, Reinhold. *The Nature and Destiny of Man.* Volumes I and II. New York: Scribner's, 1953.

Patton, John. *Is Human Forgiveness Possible?* Nashville: Abingdon, 1985

Roberts, David E. *Psychotherapy and a Christian View of Man.* New York: Scribner's, 1950.

Rogers, Carl R. *On Becoming a Person: A Therapist's View of Psychotherapy.* Boston: Houghton Mifflin, 1961.

Satir, Virginia. *Peoplemaking.* Palo Alto, CA: Science and Behavior Books, 1972.

Shakespeare, William. *The Tragedy of Macbeth.* New York: Washington Square, 1992.

Smedes, Lewis B. *Forgive & Forget: Healing the Hurts We Don't Deserve.* San Francisco: Harper & Row, 1984.

Tillich, Paul. *The Courage to Be.* New Haven: Yale University Press, 1952.

———. *The New Being.* New York: Scribner's, 1955.